D1280953

A lawyer reviews

The

Trial of

Jesus

Earle L. Wingo

Past President, Mississippi State Bar Association

CHICK
PUBLICATIONS
Ontario, Calif 91761

For a complete list of distributors near you,
call (909) 987-0771, or visit
www.chick.com

©2009 by Jack T. Chick LLC

Original edition illustrated by Jack Chick,
edited, annotated and published by:
  CHICK PUBLICATIONS
  PO Box 3500, Ontario, Calif. 91761-1019 USA
  Tel: (909) 987-0771
  Fax: (909) 941-8128
  Web: www.chick.com
  Email: postmaster@chick.com
  Printed in the United States of America

ISBN: 978-0-7589-0697-7

CONTENTS

JESUS MEASURED THE SCOPE OF HIS
SUPREME SACRIFICE WHEN HE SAID:

Greater love hath no man
than this, that a man lay down
his life for his friends.*

He came unto his own, and
his own received him not.**

*John 15:13 **John 1:11

All the factual references pertaining to the Passion of Christ were taken from the four Gospels, Matthew, Mark, Luke and John; and the Acts of the Apostles.

Quotes from the several provisions of the Hebrew laws concerning the trials of Jesus Christ came from and are amply supported by the following authorities:

- Leviticus, Numbers, Deuteronomy
- The Jewish *Talmud, Mishna*, etc.
- Innes' book *The Trial of Jesus Christ*
- Edersheim's *Life and Times of Jesus the Messiah*
- Mendelsohn's *Criminal Jurisprudence of Ancient Hebrews*
- Maimonides' *Sanhedrin IV*
- Simon Greenleaf's *Law of Evidence*
- Benny's *Criminal Code of the Jews*
- The writings of Josephus, the eminent writer of the Life of Christ.

PREFACE

Millions have read of the so-called "trial" of Jesus Christ, as briefly set forth in the Gospels of Matthew, Mark, Luke and John. Other references are recorded in the Acts of the Apostles.

Thousands of impassioned and deeply eloquent sermons have been preached on this subject. One cannot hear those accounts without concluding that the treatment of Christ was most brutal and spiteful; and that His persecutors seemed determined to magnify, in every possible manner, His suffering and humiliation.

A study of both the Hebrew and Roman trials will establish beyond any doubt that Jesus was not given even the remotest semblance of a legal trial. On the contrary, He was the victim of an unholy, mob rule persecution, which resulted in His murder.

Many of us are familiar with famous trials involving people who were placed into the spotlight of fame because of the atrociousness of the crime with which they were charged, people like Socrates, Aaron Burr, Mary Stuart, Queen of Scotland, and Warren Hastings.

We may not agree with the results of those trials, or

the degree of punishment imposed, but they were all accorded the benefit of the legal rules of orderly procedure, and the application of the laws. None were denied the substantial rights guaranteed the accused.

Moreover, proof of guilt had to be first established by competent evidence from reliable witnesses. To do less would have encouraged a state of barbarity.

Nothing could be more revolting than a court denying the accused his well-defined rights, either through ignorance, prejudice or corruption.

Sadly, quite a few innocent individuals have been convicted and sentenced to die, only to learn the truth later—when it was too late to rectify the wrong done. Such a spectacle is always heart-rending.

Mob rule is universally condemned as uncivilized. Bloodthirsty men have no sense of justice as they carry on their deeds of cowardice against helpless victims.

Many years ago, after I accepted Jesus Christ as my personal Saviour, I began an intensive study of the conditions in Judea during the life of Jesus, to understand the motives which prompted the Jewish religious groups and the members of the Roman society to maintain such an apparent hatred of Christ.

Now, I feel that others should better understand the cause for the unrest which permeated Judea when Jesus was tried before the Sanhedrin, or ecclesiastical court, and also before Pontius Pilate, the Roman Governor.

Some may excuse the Jewish leaders on the premise that the treatment accorded Jesus was in keeping with the prophecies, and that it was His will that they be fulfilled. This, however, is something God alone shall decide.

This much is unquestionably true: The Word of God relates how Jesus was subjected to two separate "trials," and was condemned to die and was later crucified.

There is raised this inquiry: Were the Jews without blame for this ordeal? According to the Gospel narratives, the Jews made the charge of blasphemy in the first trial before the Sanhedrin, the Jewish court.

They later carried Him before Pilate, the Roman Governor, where they charged Him with sedition. The Jews tried to get Pilate to approve their condemnation and sentence of death; and they demanded that Jesus be crucified. However, the final act of crucifying Jesus was done by the Romans.

But one may further inquire: Upon whom should the greater blame be charged, the Jews or the Romans?

When Pilate reminded the Master that he, Pilate, had power to order Him crucified, Jesus replied:

> Thou couldest have no power at all against me, except it were given thee from above: therefore he that delivered me unto thee hath the greater sin. [1]

No doubt, Jesus was referring to the high priest, Caiaphas, who held the loftiest position in Jewish society. This same Caiaphas led Jesus and the mob to the court of the Roman Governor, Pontius Pilate.

---

1) John 19:11.

A careful analysis of all the Jewish laws in existence when Jesus was tried brings one to the conclusion that the entire proceedings were a mockery. Every protective law was ignored when dealing with Jesus.

This review will point out the progressive steps of the ordeal, from the illegal arrest to the unlawful crucifixion, and the many wrongs deliberately committed by men who hated the Man of Galilee.

It is the hope of the author that many who read this story of His indescribable suffering and humiliations will come to the full realization that the one and only hope remaining for a restless, war-ridden, sin-cursed humanity can be found in Him as their Redeemer and Saviour. This, I believe with all of my heart:

> For God so loved the world, that he gave his only begotten Son, that whosoever believeth in him should not perish, but have everlasting life. [2]

This belief of mine has been the source of lasting consolations, bringing to me a rich experience and countless blessings which were certainly undeserved.

Earle L. Wingo

---

2) John 3:16.

CHAPTER ONE

JESUS CHRIST,
THE SON OF GOD

"For unto you is born this day in the city of David a Saviour, which is Christ the Lord." Luke 2:11

In the book of Luke, we find this beautiful story of the humble birth of Christ the Lord:

> And it came to pass in those days, that there went out a decree from Caesar Augustus, that all the world should be taxed… And all went to be taxed, every one into his own city.
>
> And Joseph also went up from Galilee, out of the city of Nazareth, into Judaea, unto the city of David, which is called Bethlehem; (because he was of the house and lineage of David:) To be taxed with Mary his espoused wife, being great with child.
>
> And so it was, that, while they were there, the days were accomplished that she should be delivered. And she brought forth her first-born son, and wrapped him in swaddling clothes, and laid him in a manger; because there was no room for them in the inn.
>
> And there were in the same country shepherds abiding in the field, keeping watch over their flock by night. And, lo, the angel of the Lord came upon them, and the glory of the Lord shone round about them: and they were sore afraid.
>
> And the angel said unto them, Fear not: for, behold, I bring you good tidings of great joy, which shall be to all people. For unto you is born this day in the city of David a Saviour, which is Christ the Lord.

> And this shall be a sign unto you; Ye shall
> find the babe wrapped in swaddling clothes,
> lying in a manger.
>
> And suddenly there was with the angel a
> multitude of the heavenly host praising God,
> and saying, Glory to God in the highest, and
> on earth peace, good will toward men. [1]

The birth of Jesus in a borrowed stable in the little village of Bethlehem began the birth of Christianity. The humble surroundings of His nativity were typical of His manner of living thereafter, for He had no desire for earthly possessions. This accounts for Him being buried in a borrowed tomb through the kindness of Joseph of Arimathaea.

A beautiful editorial titled "Jesus, the Perfect Man," concluded with this inspiring appraisal of Christ:

> Jesus spoke the truth; He lived the truth, and
> truth is eternal.
>
> The human experiences of 2,000 years show
> that Jesus never made a mistake.
>
> History has no record of any other man leading a perfect life or doing everything in logical order. Jesus is the only person whose every action and whose every utterance strikes a true note in the heart and mind of every man born of woman.
>
> No poet, no dreamer, no philosopher loved

---

1) Luke 2:1,3-14.

humanity with the love that Jesus bore toward all men.

Who, then, was Jesus?

He could not have been merely a man, for there never was a man who had two consecutive thoughts absolutely in true perfection.

Jesus m...s him to be—a Divine Being—or He could not have been what He was. No mind but an infinite mind could have left behind those things which Jesus gave to the world as a heritage. [2]

One of the most saddening revelations of the human heart is the cruel attitude of those Jewish religious leaders toward Jesus. He never did them a single wrong. Yet they repeatedly sought to entrap and humiliate Him, and finally, with equal determination, to destroy Him. Their hearts were as cold as their heads were hard.

Certainly it is a great truth that the life, character and personality of the Lowly Nazarene transcends every person of all ages. No one can be compared to Him. Even the greatest of men appear in pitiful contrast with Jesus Christ. This will remain true to the end of time.

One may easily appreciate the greatness of Jesus by reading the things He taught, and the manner in which He taught. Down through the unfolding centuries He has been truthfully called "The Great Teacher."

---

2) C.P.J. Mooney, Editorial entitled "Jesus, the Perfect Man," *Commercial Appeal*, Memphis, TN, Dec. 22, 1912.

The confession of Simon Peter was the true affirmation of the New Testament when he said: *"Thou art the Christ, the Son of the living God."*[3] Moreover, it explained the life of Jesus and His reign in the hearts of Christian men and women since the advent of His earthly ministry.

Further confirmation of His Divine nature came from the voice of God. When Jesus was baptized by John, God spoke up and said: *"This is my beloved Son, in whom I am well pleased."*[4] Then again at the transfiguration, the same voice of God said: *"This is my beloved Son: hear him."*[5]

And what about His absolute dominance over the forces which produce death? This alone is ample proof of His Divinity and His being truly the Son of God. Yes, His command to Lazarus to *"come forth"*[6] alive from a four-day-old grave was far more than mere magic—it was the revelation of the power of God.

In considering the life of Jesus, and His great character, we must never overlook the fact that, while He was truly Divine, He was also human. There reposed in His heart a deep and abiding love for a lost world. He shared His Father's redemptive purpose. His willingness to publicly identify Himself with known sinners and publicans, and to share their shame of iniquity, shows the unmeasured compassion which He always bore towards all of them. Never did He turn a deaf ear to a plea for relief of distress or pain.

---

3) See Matthew 16:16.
4) See Matthew 3:17.
5) See Mark 9:7; Luke 9:35; Matthew 17:5 and 2 Peter 1:17.
6) See John 11:43.

As we read of His willing sacrifice on the rugged cross for the sins of mankind, we find the world's most beautiful example of unswerving devotion to the Father's will. It was positive evidence of heroic, sustained courage and triumphant faith. With Him, there was never a thought of turning back from the bitter ordeal of inhuman torture, to which He knew He would be subjected. Obedience to the will of His Father was His only desire.

While Jesus was upon this earth, He plainly enumerated the high cost of discipleship. When someone glibly offered to follow Him, Jesus reminded him:

> The foxes have holes, and the birds of the
> air have nests; but the Son of man hath not
> where to lay his head.[7]

This was certainly no promise of a life of ease, but rather one of great sacrificing and privation in a spirit of unselfishness and abiding humility.

As may be expected, uncounted thousands were so closely wedded to the relationships of the world that they were unwilling to renounce those ties and follow Him.

Others found His words hard to understand, and His standards of human conduct too severe and too hard to accept. They were like the rich young ruler of Biblical days, who refused to give up his earthly accumulations, and turned from His majestic leadership to drift back into the ways of commonplace existence—soon to be forever forgotten and lost amid the hurly-burly of sinful men.

---

7) See Matthew 8:20; Luke 9:58.

The great love which Jesus bore for all humanity was truly without parallel. His eternal compassion for the lame, the sick, the blind, and even the wretched sinner, knew no bounds. His hands were ever ready to heal, and His heart ever ready to forgive.

This was Christ whom the Jews, in the year AD 30, spat upon, ridiculed, scourged, crowned with thorns, and brutally nailed to a cross to die. After experiencing the untold agony of inhuman brutality, and while conscious that earthly life would last but a short while longer, this same Jesus, with blood-filled eyes and parched lips, raised His head in the direction of His Heavenly Father and uttered a fervent prayer of pardon for His brutal murderers:

> Father, forgive them; for they know not what they do. [8]

Shortly afterwards, the Master declared:

> It is finished: [9] Father, into thy hands I commend my spirit… [10]

Even in the fleeting, last moments of life, Jesus was mindful of great compassion and His unfailing sense of forgiveness.

---

8) See Luke 23:34.
9) See John 19:30.
10) See Luke 23:46.

CHAPTER 2

PRE-TRIAL DAYS
IN JUDEA

To more fully appreciate the reasons for the brutal treatment of Jesus, it would be well to set forth a brief sketch of the tumultuous conditions which existed at that time in Judea.

A glance at the political scene reveals that the Jews had gone through a process of slow successions and were completely dominated by the Assyrians, Babylonians, Persians, Greeks and finally the Romans.

It was while the Jews were under the domination of the Romans that Herod the Great, a criminal and murderer, ascended to the throne in Judea. This arch scalawag disgraced his high office until his death in 4 BC.

Then the country was divided into three districts, known as tetrarchies, with each under the command of a tetrarch. They later became known as procurators. In the year 6 AD, all Judea became a Roman province and was governed by procurators sent out from Rome.

The political situation in Judea at that time was quite complicated and anomalous in many respects, having undergone frequent changes, but retaining certain peculiarities which made the country unique among the other dependencies of Rome. They were allowed, for a short time, to maintain a degree of semi-independence.

However, there frequently arose serious disputes as to the limitations which had been imposed, since there does not appear to have been any specific treaty defining the mutual rights and obligations existing between the two powers.

Tiberius
Caesar

Herod

Pontius Pilate

Caiaphas

Annas

Judea was subject to the whims of Rome, and whenever Roman interests required, the Roman authorities interfered in matters of legislation and administration.

Since the Romans were the conquerors and the Jews were the conquered, their religious and political freedoms were lost. The beliefs and creeds of the Jews degenerated into burdensome observances which were strictly imposed by their high priests, scribes and rulers.

Tiberius Caesar, the Roman Emperor, was the political master of both Herod and Pontius Pilate. Although Caesar was the real procurator, or governor, of Judea, Pilate served in that capacity during the time of the trial of Jesus, as a substitute for the emperor in that area. Every word and deed of Pilate was subject to the approval of Caesar, whose displeasure Pilate was always keen to avoid.

Because of the comparatively short terms allowed those political appointees, together with the frivolous reasons for their dismissal, we can readily account for the cowardice and vacillating attitude of Pilate at a time when there was a great need for moral courage and independent action.

One of the loftiest positions held by a Jew in Palestine was high priest. He was the presiding judge of the Jewish court, known as the Sanhedrin, which consisted of seventy-one members of the Jewish society. Caiaphas served as high priest when Jesus was tried. We shall discuss him later.

Two Religious Groups

There were two principal religious groups in Judea, the Sadducees and the Pharisees.

The Sadducees were dominated by a man named Annas, the deposed high priest, whose son-in-law was the appointed high priest. This group did not believe in the resurrection, nor rewards or punishment in a life beyond the grave. With them, all ended at death. All of their beliefs ran counter to what Jesus was teaching and practicing.

SADDUCEES
Did not believe in
the resurrection

PHARISEES
Did ▬ believe in
the resurrection

The Pharisees were an arrogant group, filled with hypocrisy, who seemed pleased to give free counsel in their "better-than-thou" attitudes of false piety. Tradition and custom were everything with them.

The Sadducees won a measure of confidence from those in power, and thus received from the Romans the highest positions within the Sanhedrin. As a result, almost ninety percent of the Sanhedrin was made up of Sadducees.

Petty jealousies, suspicions and lust for more power and greater prominence were rampant among these two religious groups. Almost everywhere, one could observe the grim evidence of selfishness written upon the countenances of even the humblest Jews.

Also, it was well known that both the Sadducees and the Pharisees maintained a secret contempt for their Roman rulers. No wonder there was confusion, distrust and hatred in the air.

It was Paul of Tarsus, the great convert, whose words fit the description of the two Jewish religious groups:

> Being filled with all unrighteousness, fornication, wickedness, covetousness, maliciousness; full of envy, murder, debate, deceit, malignity; whisperers, Backbiters, haters of God, despiteful, proud, boasters, inventors of evil things, disobedient to parents, Without understanding, covenant breakers, without natural affection, implacable, unmerciful:[11]

---

11) See Romans 1:29-31.

What a stinging and yet truthful indictment against the religious groups and leaders in Judea at the time of Christ. Paul knew whereof he spoke, for he lived among and preached to them for several years. He could accuse them because he had seen the evidence himself.

Later chapters will show that the bitterest opponents of Jesus were these two religious sects, and that they could never see eye to eye with, or understand the teachings of Christ. We will also show that they never lost an opportunity to vent their hatred of Him, as they sought to humiliate and embarrass the Lowly Nazarene—but always to no avail.

It was into this highly discordant, wicked and turbulent state of affairs within the Jewish society in the year AD 27, that Jesus of Nazareth, the sinless, humble and meek son of a carpenter, brought His great message of forgiveness of sins and the promise of eternal life to all mankind.

CHAPTER 3

JEWISH HOPES FOR AN EARTHLY KING

For several hundred years before the birth of Christ, the priests and scribes taught the Jews to look forward to the coming of a Messiah, an earthly king who would restore them to a position of power and prosperity, and re-establish the earthly kingdom of David.

This would relieve them of the heavy burdens of taxation so ruthlessly imposed upon them by their Roman conquerors. Their hearts longed for the great day when He would arrive.

As a captive people, they had lost all pride, but this Messianic expectation was the one thing they could look forward to. Often, in their eagerness, they were misled into believing that their long expected Messiah had come among them. Still they maintained hope that he would soon redeem them from the bonds of slavery and give to each a life of ease and splendor.

When John the Baptist began his crusade for repentance and spoke so fervently of the coming day of judgment, the Jews, their hopes aflame, began whispering that this man was the long-awaited Messiah. But John firmly refuted their speculations, adding that he was merely a voice in the wilderness, preparing the way for the coming of the real Messiah. To add a note of encouragement, John said:

> I baptize with water: but there standeth one
> among you, whom ye know not; He it is, who
> coming after me is preferred before me, whose
> shoe's latchet I am not worthy to unloose. [12]

When Jesus miraculously fed the five thousand men with five barley loaves and two small fishes, they crowded about Him and virtually demanded that He be crowned their king, then and there. But since His kingdom was not of this earth, He bade them depart for their homes, as He went alone into the mountains to pray. [13]

---

12) John 1:26-27.
13) See John 6:1-15.

The resistance of Jesus to becoming their earthly king weakened the effect of the great miracle of the feeding which they had just witnessed, and was the first turning of the tide of popular enthusiasm for Him. They felt that if He were really the expected Messiah, He should have let them proclaim Him their earthly king.

The Jews were not happy. Through their darkest hours, there was a full allotment of prophets and other religious leaders who constantly reminded them that hope was not lost, and that God would soon relieve them of their misery.

The Jews had prayed for a Kingdom of God—not in righteousness, joy and peace in the Holy Ghost—but in meat and drink. They cherished the thought of and insisted upon a kingdom on earth which would rival all others; one which would produce a miraculous triumph over their despised Roman rulers.

Therefore, on the day after their efforts to make Jesus their earthly king failed, the vast majority of His followers either remained in their homes or went toward Jerusalem to celebrate the Feast of the Passover. They simply could not understand Christ's refusal to be the means of fulfilling their highest hopes. Jesus repeatedly explained to them that His kingdom was not of this earth, and that they should:

> Labour not for the meat which perisheth, but for that meat which endureth unto everlasting life, which the Son of man shall give unto you: [14]

---

14) John 6:27.

Despite this promise, they turned away from Him by the uncounted thousands, and refused to believe that which He so plainly taught and preached. This was a totally different Messiah and Messianic Kingdom than that which they conceived and wished for.

One can easily imagine the great joy in the hearts of those Jews when they thought there was a chance to proclaim a miracle-man as their earthly king. This kind of a king, they reasoned, would cure all who suffered with physical ailments, and even bring the dead back to life.

With such a king there would be no death among the Jews, no pain, no suffering, no disappointments. Life would be perfect. The trouble was that their only concern was for the carnal rather than the spiritual.

Jesus assured the Jews more than once, *"I am the bread of life:"*[15] and to share in that food was to have everlasting life.[16] Unfortunately, they did not understand His words.

This was the regrettable parting of the ways between Jesus and most of His followers. And it was all because they failed to understand the truth of His wonderful words.

Scripture tells the story in a few words:

> From that time many of his disciples went
> back, and walked no more with him.[17]

The disappointment was mutual because their desertion of Him in a crucial hour of His ministry also broke His Heart.

---

15) See John 6:35.
16) See John 6:32-51.
17) John 6:66.

Yes, the crucial hour of decision was past, and the hand upon the silent dial of destiny was pointing to the hour of His death.

When consideration is given to the great turmoil and stress of the days to follow, it will be well to keep in mind that most of the trouble came from this hope of the Jews for an earthly king. To the very last hours of His life on this earth, His closest followers—His disciples—still thought He would consent to be their ***earthly king!***

CHAPTER 4

MAIN CHARACTERS AGAINST JESUS

The following men actively participated in the tragic and cowardly crucifixion of Christ:

JUDAS ISCARIOT, one of the disciples, who betrayed his Master and best friend for thirty pieces of silver.

ANNAS, a Sadducee, the political boss of Judea, before whom Jesus was first taken after the arrest.

29

CAIAPHAS, a Sadducee, the son-in-law of Annas, and the high priest who presided over the Jewish trial of Jesus.

PONTIUS PILATE, Governor of Judea, before whom Jesus was taken twice for trial, and who, though finding Him not guilty four separate times, turned Him over to the mob to be crucified.

HEROD, the Tetrarch of Galilee, before whom Jesus was also taken for trial.

TIBERIUS CAESAR, holder of the high office of Emperor of Rome during the "trials" of Jesus. He appointed Pontius Pilate to the office of Governor of Judea.

THE GREAT SANHEDRIN, located in Jerusalem, was the highest Jewish religious court, and consisted of seventy-one members, including the high priest, who was the presiding officer. Jesus was first tried for "blasphemy" before this court.

THE SADDUCEES, a religious group that predominated in the membership of the Jewish court.

THE PHARISEES, another religious group, who followed traditions and rituals rather than the laws of God.

THE UNRULY, CRUEL MOB of ingrates who persecuted and finally crucified Jesus Christ.

We shall now take up, in the above order, the ten principal actors in that awful drama involving Jesus:

Judas Iscariot

When one thinks of a dastardly betrayer, the name Judas, one of the supposedly loyal disciples of Jesus, comes to mind. It was he who planted the betrayer's kiss upon the cheek of his Master.

> Then one of the twelve, called Judas Iscariot, went unto the chief priests, And said unto them, What will ye give me, and I will deliver him unto you? And they covenanted with him for thirty pieces of silver. And from that time he sought opportunity to betray him. [18]
>
> Now he that betrayed him gave them a sign, saying, Whomsoever I shall kiss, that same is

---

18) Matthew 26:14-16.

he: hold him fast. And forthwith he came to
Jesus, and said, Hail, master; and kissed him. [19]

Thus was the unholy bargain sealed and completed. Judas waited until after the midnight hour near the garden of Gethsemane, to betray his Master. That was the arranged signal for which the Roman soldiers and temple guards had waited. Without further ceremony they seized and bound Jesus like a long hunted desperado, and took Him in chains to Annas for trial.

Judas hailed from Kerioth in Judea, and was the only Judean among the disciples. He had been repeatedly honored by Jesus by being sent on holy missions; was given the power to cast out devils, and was appointed treasurer of the little group of disciples.

Why then was he so eager to deliver his Master into the hands of sinful men? The love for money was his undoing. He became greatly disappointed when he realized that Jesus had no intention of setting up an earthly kingdom. [20] He also witnessed the refusal of Jesus to accede to the demands of His followers to be their king, and He saw Jesus beginning to effect a realignment along spiritual lines.

Worldly pomp and power was his dream, and realizing that such was not in the plans of the Master, he assumed an attitude of resentment and bitterness for the spiritual program of Christ. He felt that he was following a pauper rather than an earthly king.

Satan filled his heart as he determined to get what he

---

19) Matthew 26:48-49.
20) Jesus' kingdom is "not of this world" (John 18:36).

could for the betrayal of Jesus. When the soldiers, led by Judas, told Jesus who they were seeking, and Christ replied, *"I am he,"*[21] they went backward, and fell to the ground.[22]

It took them several moments to regain their composure before proceeding with the unlawful arrest. From that moment on, Judas was filled with deep shame and remorse, for he soon thereafter admitted having played the fool.

The human heart can experience no greater sting than that of justified remorse of conscience. Judas knew well that there would never be any redemption. He was lost amid the catacombs of desolate and despised men. What happened to this arch betrayer?

> Then Judas, which had betrayed him, when he saw that he was condemned, repented himself, and brought again the thirty pieces of silver to the chief priests and elders, Saying, I have sinned in that I have betrayed the innocent blood. And they said, What is that to us? see thou to that. And he cast down the pieces of silver in the temple, and departed, and went and hanged himself.[23]

Yes, Judas willingly confessed that he had sinned by betraying Christ, his loyal and best friend and benefactor.

No wonder the world's most despicable traitor placed a rope about his neck and committed suicide.

What a grim spectacle. A wretched, hopeless betrayer

---

21) John 18:5.
22) See John 18:6.
23) Matthew 27:3-5.

dangling from the end of a rope that all might behold the result of his despair. What a reminder of the extreme penalty which was self-inflicted by one whose lust for money outweighed all sense of self-respect and decency. His attitude was confession of wrong without repentance.

After almost two thousand years, his cowardly deed of treachery remains fresh in the hearts of billions who regard his name as a symbol of shame and disgrace. No greater insult could be hurled at another than to say he is a "Judas."

Jesus was renowned for speaking out in plain terms either praise or condemnation. In all of the Master's many expressions, none are more stinging than His appraisal of Judas Iscariot, His betrayer:

> The Son of man indeed goeth, as it is written
> of him: but woe to that man by whom the
> Son of man is betrayed! good were it for that
> man if he had never been born. [24]

Annas, The Political Boss of Judea

In the year 7 AD the procurator, Coponius, appointed his friend, Annas, the son of Seth, an Alexandrian Sadducee as the high priest at Jerusalem, the highest appointive office of Jewry.

The high priestly family of Annas held full sway, with only a few brief interruptions, for the following fifty-one years. All six of his sons followed their father as high priest during that long period of time, and it was his son-in-law, Caiaphas, who, through the dominant influence of this

---

24) Mark 14:21.

same Annas, held that high office during the time when Jesus was tried before the Sanhedrin in AD 30.

Although Annas was a feeble man in his late eighties, he possessed great wealth and political power in Jerusalem. He was their political boss and his every thought, word and deed conveyed the height of his extreme egotism.

It was generally admitted that old Annas had the most superb intelligence among the ruling elements in all Judea; and he seemed unacquainted with fear or remorse of conscience. His tyrannical and unholy philosophy was that of "rule or ruin."

He was quite generous in providing numerous luxuries for his son-in-law, and was never timid about reminding Caiaphas of the lasting and unpaid debt of gratitude he was owed. Therefore, it was not unusual for Caiaphas to unfailingly do the bidding of his father-in-law, regardless of ethics, law, morals, or any consequences.

Annas could not be called a religious man. Being a devout Sadducee, he openly subscribed to the creed that there was no life after death, and no spiritual world. He taught that future rewards and punishments were absurd, and that everything ended at the grave.

Annas regarded everything Jesus taught as nothing more than the abstractions of a discredited, false prophet. He had no patience with nor respect for the new, religious theories of the Master.

He had a deep motive, as he thought, for conspiring with Caiaphas and money-mad Judas Iscariot to speedily get rid of the Lowly Nazarene, regardless of the means to that end. Murder was commonplace with this corrupt individual, and he entertained no scruples about engaging in evil enterprises if he could accomplish what he desired.

It is noteworthy that those who sold the doves and lambs in the Temple to be burned upon the altars of sacrifice were the hirelings of Annas. His bankers also profited by the usurious exchange of Roman currency into the coinage of the Temple.

They were there to enrich the already fat purse of their employer; and Annas saw no wrong with having them engage in such unholy practices in the Temple, for he considered the Temple nothing more than a convenient meeting place, where crowds congregated for their religious practices, and where the unfair exchanges would be made to his personal benefit.

What a sight. Droves of poor Jews, trudging daily into the Temple to offer their sacrifices, having to purchase lambs and doves, and exchange their coins with Annas' agents, since he had a monopoly on that sordid business.

Annas, like countless thousands in Judea, heard of the miracles of Jesus; especially His raising Lazarus from the grave. That greatly irritated the old man. He now looked ridiculous before his followers because of all his preaching and teaching that life after death was nonsense.

There was no denying that this event occurred, since it was witnessed by hundreds of reputable Jews, who quickly spread the news throughout the land.

In his declining years, Annas was forced to admit that his conclusions about the resurrection had been repudiated by this humble Man from Galilee. With his prestige on the wane, something had to be done, and quickly, to dispose of this troublemaker whose miracles and teachings were the source of a deep-rooted embarrassment.

To increase the consuming fire of enmity, word reached Annas that Jesus had bodily forced his money-changers and dove and lamb sellers out of the Temple, and into the busy streets of Jerusalem, dodging the sturdy lashes from the whip in the strong arm of Jesus.

Annas was outraged, humiliated, and determined to get even. The cleansing of the Temple was considered a direct challenge to the authority of Annas and his Sadducees. They determined to retaliate.

It was shortly after this episode that Annas and Caiaphas entered into the sordid and unholy conspiracy with Judas Iscariot to betray the Master.

John tells us where Jesus was first taken after His unlawful arrest outside the Garden of Gethsemane:

> Then the band and the captain and officers
> of the Jews took Jesus, and bound him, And
> led him away to Annas first; for he was father
> in law to Caiaphas, which was the high priest
> that same year. [25]

Taking Jesus to Annas first was no coincidence. It had been planned that way. Having knowledge of the arrest of Jesus was all Annas needed. He could then secretly arrange with Caiaphas, the high priest, to quickly call a nighttime

---

25) John 18:12-13. See also John 11:49.

meeting of the Sanhedrin, create a quorum of only twenty-three carefully-chosen members, then begin the trial of Christ and terminate His ministry by condemning Him to death while His friends were still asleep. That is exactly what they did.

Annas, devoid of principle and with a heart black to the core, willingly connived with Judas and Caiaphas for the cold-blooded murder of the Son of God.

Caiaphas, The High Priest

Of all the men involved in the trials and crucifixion of Christ, Caiaphas, the high priest, was the most despicable. In saying this, we are mindful of the treachery of Judas Iscariot. To be sure, the high priest was more corrupt.

For eleven years, from 25 to 36 AD, he held that lofty position in Judea, and was devoid of ethics or even common decency. His close friendship with Pontius Pilate, the Roman Governor, was grounded upon their common proposition, a deep hatred for Christ, whose teachings they scoffed with an abiding venom. Both were political cowards—men who dreaded the thought of having their heads removed from the public trough.

As the presiding judge of the Sanhedrin, Caiaphas was required to take a solemn oath under the Jewish laws to always assume an attitude of impartiality toward every accused person brought before the court. He was to manifest complete indifference as to the results of any trial; and he would not serve as the presiding officer should a case arise in which he bore enmity toward the accused.

Unable to hide his deep hatred of Jesus Christ, we find him, even before the arrest was made, conspiring to murder Christ—and seeking false witnesses to appear before the court. But that is not the end of his corruption.

Next this judge personally charges Jesus with "blasphemy," then has the gall to announce in open court that there is no need for witnesses.

As further evidence of his utter unfitness and lack of judicial temperament, he tears his own garments from his shoulders to his waistband. Matthew records how Caiaphas conducted himself:

> Then the high priest rent his clothes, saying, He hath spoken blasphemy; what further need have we of witnesses? behold, now ye have heard his blasphemy. What think ye? They answered and said, He is guilty of death. [26]

---

26) Matthew 26:65-66.

When Jesus gave an affirmative answer as to whether He was the Christ, the Son of God, He was denounced as a blasphemer. Utterly ridiculous.

With the approval of this same high priest, the members of the court, in complete disregard for existing laws, spit in the face of Jesus and buffeted Him. Others smote Him with the palms of their hands, saying, *"Prophesy unto us, thou Christ, Who is he that smote thee?"*[27]

Despite this display of rage and ill-will, the high priest was not yet contented. He next led the bound and bleeding Christ over to the palace of Pilate, hoping to obtain a speedy approval of their unholy and unlawful verdict that Christ should die because of blasphemy.

Before the procession started its journey for the second trial, they placed a sharp crown of thorns upon the head of the Master and struck several blows upon His head to insure the deep imbedding of the thorns into His brow.[28] Hence, He was led to Pilate with His eyes filled with blood.

What a "judge." What a "trial." Somewhere in the old Jewish law there is this wise and true maxim:

> A disreputable and corrupt judge is to be no more respected than the sweat from the blanket of a jackass.

Indeed, Judas Iscariot betrayed his best friend for filthy silver, and in remorse, hanged himself. But Caiaphas committed the greater sin. He forever disgraced the office of

27) See Matthew 26:67-68.
28) See Matthew 27:29-30; Mark 15:17-18; and John 19:2-3.

high priesthood through his vile conduct as the presiding official in the supreme court of Jewry. Moreover, he became a deliberate law-violator in the following respects:

1. He knew that his heart was filled with poisonous enmity for Jesus, but he continued to preside at that trial, after taking an oath that he had no enmity toward the accused.

2. His oath to be fair and impartial was made a mockery when he admitted being a party to the corrupt conspiracy with Annas and Judas to have Jesus betrayed.

3. He raped the law when he made the charge of "blasphemy" after Jesus admitted being the Son of God.

4. He winked at justice and blinded his eyes to fairness when he searched for those false witnesses.

5. Being learned in the law, which was a prerequisite to his assuming the duties of that high office, he pretended ignorance of the law which required two witnesses, whose testimony must be in agreement as to all material details embracing the charge against the accused.

6. He ignored the Jewish legal mandates that no trial be held at night, nor during the feast of the Passover, or on the day before a Sabbath.

7. Caiaphas himself called for the vote of the death penalty, and unlawfully recorded it, when the Jewish law prohibited the death sentence. Long before, the Roman conquerors had denied them such authority.

8. He painted a picture of bestiality and contempt by deliberately tearing his own robe in the courtroom, and then permitting his cowardly cohorts to spit in the face of

the prisoner, to strike Him, and ridicule Him with other modes of cruelty, such as forcing into His brow that thorn-covered crown as a mock symbol of Kingship.

It was Caiaphas who, before Pilate, raised the loudest voice for the release of Barabbas, and for the demand that Jesus be crucified. Still not appeased, he gave minute directions to the Roman soldiers for the commission of further acts of brutality while Jesus was suspended on the cross.

One can easily get a mental picture of the smirking Caiaphas as Christ begged for water to cool His parched throat, but received instead a sponge soaked in vinegar.

How do you suppose the high priest felt on that fateful afternoon when, standing at the foot of the cross, he heard the dying Christ's fervent prayer for forgiveness because His murderers knew not what they were doing?[29]

Imagine the reaction of Caiaphas when the earth quaked and the lightning struck; and he knew that Jesus had died; and he heard one of the murderers, a Roman soldier say: *"Truly this was the Son of God."*[30]

The world will ever remember with justified disgust the sad spectacle of that vicious, immoral, inhuman, cowardly, prejudiced, disreputable "judge" of the highest Jewish court who delighted in leading the frenzied mob in its base acts of brutality and cold-blooded murder.

---

29) See Luke 23:34.
30) See Matthew 27:54 and Mark 15:39.

Pontius Pilate, Governor of Judea

Pilate was a native of Seville, one of the larger cities in Spain, where all of the inhabitants enjoyed the coveted rights of Roman citizens. History tells us that he was a vile traitor to the cause of the Spaniards. When Spain fell to the greatly superior Roman warriors, his father served as a famous general on the side of the Romans. Shortly thereafter, he married 15-year-old Claudia, the youngest daughter of Julia, the only child of Augustus Caesar.

Julia, Pilate's mother-in-law, had married several others, including the present emperor, Tiberius Caesar. So Pilate had married the step-granddaughter of the Roman Emperor.

Later, because of this marriage, Pilate was appointed procurator, or Governor, of Judea, by the then Emperor, Tiberius Caesar.

Pilate was a man of extreme violence, who frequently

delighted in causing much ill-treatment to many of the Jews within his jurisdiction. It is recorded that he alone was responsible for the execution of hundreds of innocent Jews. Being the Governor of Judea, he had full jurisdiction over the civil, criminal and military matters within his domain; and answered only to the Emperor for the welfare and behavior of the Jews within Judea.

While he had no love for the Jews, he feared the possibility that some of them might report him to his political benefactor, the Emperor, and obtain his removal from that high office. Many of his predecessors had been removed for slight causes. Thus, he kept his ear to the ground for any rumblings of dissension over the way he conducted the affairs of State.

Once, when he was warned that a group of Jewish citizens planned to complain to him over his harsh treatment of them, he had a band of his soldiers conceal large knives under their garments, and when the helpless group came within reach, he gave the signal and they were brutally stabbed to death.

Since Jesus was a Jew, Pilate had no reason to entertain malice toward Him. He just did not like any Jew. But during the second "trial" of Christ before Pilate, the Governor showed no evidence of enmity. On the contrary, he tried four separate times to release the Master by stating that he had found Him guilty of no wrongdoing.

The authors of the four Gospels, Matthew, Mark, Luke and John, place a sense of mercy into the heart of Pilate, revealing his temporary unwillingness to have any part of the crucifixion. Still, we cannot overlook the important observation that Pilate, when courage and honor were at stake, showed the pallid flag of fear by vacillating and finally giving in to the demands of the mob that Christ be surrendered to them for crucifixion.

Yet, when the time came for Pilate to assume an important role in the most powerful drama in all the world, he revealed his craven cowardice. He had the great fault of playing to the demands of the mob, and sacrificing his self-respect and power of office through fear of retaliation. He lost control of his merciful impulses when threats to report him to the Emperor were imminent. He didn't have the moral courage to stand his ground.

According to popular legend, the Emperor became greatly alarmed over the darkness which enveloped the Roman world at the moment of the crucifixion of Christ. He then ordered Pilate to proceed to Rome and explain his conduct toward Jesus. As a result of this investigation, Pilate was condemned to die as a vile murderer of an Innocent Man. The sting of blame and the penalty for playing the role of a coward cost Pilate his life.

Herod Antipas, Tetrarch of Galilee

Herod the Great, "King of the Jews," [31] married ten different women, then murdered seven of them when he became bored with their company.

He was noted for his cruelty and for being despised by his subjects. With that kind of a father, one could not ex-

---

31) In 40 BC the Roman senate elected Herod "King of the Jews."

pect much from his son, Herod Antipas. In many respects, he followed the pattern set by his father.

Herod Antipas was an individual who was without conscience, whose chief pastime was the gratification of his passions. He bore neither respect nor love for anyone. Self-ishness enveloped his entire being.

It was he who caused the beheading of John the Baptist (to pacify the whim and fancy of Salome, whose mother had married Antipas) because John dared expose the un-holy marriage and licentious conduct of this new Emperor. His lustful desires toward Salome caused him to willfully murder the forerunner of Christ.

Upon the death of Herod the Great, a last will and tes-tament was discovered, which divided the kingdom among his three sons. Herod Antipas received an annual bounty of many talents, and became king of the provinces of Perea and Galilee.

Except for the provisions of his father's will, Antipas would never have had the chance to disgrace the office of king of that domain because he was never the choice of even a small minority of the unhappy people he governed with great cruelty as a heartless tyrant.

This king of Galilee was a habitual drunkard. He daily consumed more than a gallon of hard wine, on average. No act was too low or mean as he sought pleasure in debase-ment.

He was despised by the people because of his insatiable lust and his greed for the sensual things of life. On one oc-casion, Christ was met by a group of Pharisees who warned

Him that unless He immediately left Galilee, Herod would put Him to death. Jesus replied:

> Go ye, and tell that fox, Behold, I cast out devils, and I do cures to day and to morrow, and the third day I shall be perfected. [32]

This was the same Herod before whom Pilate sent Christ, when he learned that Jesus was of Nazareth, and would come under the jurisdiction of Herod.

Regarding the "trials" of Jesus, the part played by Herod was not of much significance, so we shall dismiss him with this comment: His greatest blessing, though undeserved, was that he was one day allowed to be in the immediate presence of the living Son of God.

Tiberius Caesar, The Roman Emperor

During the "trials" of Jesus, Tiberius Caesar was the Emperor of Rome.

Under Roman laws, any Roman citizen, having been found guilty of any offense, had the right to appeal directly to the Emperor. The famous convert, Paul, had this privilege after his conviction. But since Jesus was not a Roman citizen, he did not have this right of appeal.

In reality, the Emperor played no significant part in the "trials" of Christ, but he had the power to summarily remove Pilate from office. Being a political puppet of the Emperor, Pilate was sorely afraid of his political boss in Rome, and kept constantly on guard so he might not offend him.

---

32) Luke 13:32.

The Sanhedrin, or Highest Jewish Court

The Hebrew courts were divided into three separate types: The Great Sanhedrin; the Minor Sanhedrin; and the Lower Sanhedrin.

The Great Sanhedrin was the highest court of the Jews, located in Jerusalem, and consisted of seventy-one members. The high priest was the presiding officer.

Many eminent historians agree that the Great Sanhedrin had its origin back in the wilderness with Moses, who acted under divine authority:

> …Gather unto me seventy men of the elders of Israel, whom thou knowest to be the elders of the people, and officers over them; and bring them unto the tabernacle of the congregation, that they may stand there with thee. And I … will take of the spirit which is upon thee, and will put it upon them; and they shall bear the burden of the people with thee, that thou bear it not thyself alone. [33]

Moses formerly presided over that body of seventy elders, making seventy-one, the correct number of the Great Sanhedrin. It stood the same way when Jesus was being tried.

Each member was required to possess the following qualifications before being permitted to serve:

1. He had to be a Hebrew and a lineal descendent of Hebrew parents.

---

[33] Numbers 11:16-17

2. He had to be learned in the Hebrew laws, both written and unwritten.[34]
3. He had to be familiar with the languages of the surrounding nations.
4. He had to be modest, popular, of good appearance, and free from haughtiness.
5. He had to be pious, strong, and courageous.
6. No man was qualified to sit as judge who was interested in a matter to be adjudicated.
7. He had to take an oath to be fair, and not serve where there existed enmity between him and anyone brought before the court for trial.

There was a provision to the effect that twenty-three members would constitute a quorum of the Great Sanhedrin. The high priest, as the presiding judge, could lawfully assemble the court of seventy-one by securing the presence of at least twenty-three members.

Under the rules of the *Mishnah*, a very unusual provision was made: "A unanimous verdict of guilty, rendered on the day of the trial, had the effect of an acquittal."

According to the Hebrew law, both Talmudic and Mosaic, at least two witnesses were required to convict an accused person; and at least two of the witnesses had to agree in detail as to the charge made against the prisoner.

---

34) These are known as the Written Torah and the Oral Torah. Many Jews believe the Oral Torah was written down in a 200 AD document called the Mishnah. This was combined with rabbinic commentaries (called Gemara) into a huge book about 500 AD called the Talmud. There are two Talmuds: Jerusalem and Babylonian. The Babylonian is the larger one and the one people usually mean when saying, "the Talmud."

Moreover, the Hebrew law did not permit a conviction to be based upon a confession alone. There also had to be supporting evidence.

During the "trials" of Jesus, all Judea was under strict Roman domination. But to lend a bit of flattery to its Jewish subjects, in matters of religion, they were permitted to continue operating, and be governed by, their own religious courts, known as the Sanhedrins.

The Roman conquerors had stripped the Sanhedrin of the power to impose the penalty of death. Death penalty cases had to be referred to the Governor, Pilate, for approval before such a sentence could have any effect.

It is interesting that when Jesus was tried, there were no lawyers to defend those charged with a crime. The judges performed all of the duties of the modern-day lawyer.

The Arrogant Sadducees

The Sadducees, a religious group who flourished during the ministry of Jesus, were the political aristocrats, and the wealthiest elements among the Jewish society. They maintained undisputed control over local government as well as the Great Sanhedrin.

Their wealth came principally from the commercial side of the Temple services, which involved the sale of lambs and cattle for offering of sacrifices, and the exchange of Roman for Jewish currencies, at large profits. The former high priest Annas, their political boss, placed his hired agents in the Temple for those unholy purposes.

This group did not believe in the creed of future rewards and punishments; and they taught that there was no such thing as a resurrection. [35] With them, all things ended at the grave. Hence their open animosity toward Christ who, on more than one occasion, brought the dead back to life. They scoffed at Jesus' assurances that after His death He would arise on the third day.

While the Sadducees were never very friendly with the opposing religious group, the Pharisees, the two were ever ready to combine their miserable talents in a conspiracy to destroy Christ. Enmity toward Jesus was the one thing they had in common. All that Jesus taught ran counter to the teachings of both the Sadducees and Pharisees.

When the Pharisees failed to trap Jesus into stating that it was not lawful to pay tribute to Caesar, [36] the Sadducees sent a group from their sect for the same purpose:

> The same day came to him the Sadducees, which say that there is no resurrection, and asked him, Saying, Master, Moses said, If a man die, having no children, his brother shall marry his wife, and raise up seed unto his brother.
>
> Now there were with us seven brethren: and the first, when he had married a wife, deceased, and, having no issue, left his wife unto his brother: Likewise the second also, and the third, unto the seventh. And last of all the woman died also.

---

35) See Matthew 22:23; Mark 12:18; Luke 20:27 & Acts 23:8.
36) See Matthew 22:17; Mark 12:14; & Luke 20:22.

> Therefore in the resurrection whose wife
> shall she be of the seven? for they all had her. [37]

Jesus well knew that this group had ridiculed His teachings in respect to the resurrection, and that they were not in good faith in acting upon such a premise:

> Jesus answered and said unto them, Ye do err,
> not knowing the scriptures, nor the power
> of God. For in the resurrection they neither
> marry, nor are given in marriage, but are as
> the angels of God in heaven. But as touching
> the resurrection of the dead, have ye not read
> that which was spoken unto you by God,
> saying, I am the God of Abraham, and the
> God of Isaac, and the God of Jacob? God is
> not the God of the dead, but of the living. [38]

When the multitude heard this, they were greatly astonished at His doctrine. But when the Pharisees heard that He had put the Sadducees to silence, they no longer wanted to ask Him further questions.

> And no man was able to answer him a word,
> neither durst any man from that day forth
> ask him any more questions. [39]

Failing in every attempt to trap Christ, they determined to end His ministry through a scheme and conspiracy by seeking false witnesses that "they might destroy him." [40]

---

37) Matthew 22:23-28.
38) Matthew 22:29-32.
39) Matthew 22:46.
40) See Matthew 12:14; Mark 3:6; & 11:18.

The raising of Lazarus back to life[41] and the chasing of the money-changers from the Temple of God[42] were the two acts that made the Sadducees exceedingly angry with Christ. Therefore, eager to retaliate, they happily joined forces with the Pharisees in the common cause of murdering the totally innocent Jesus. The leaders in that unholy conspiracy and cowardly alliance were the Sadducees.

The Hypocritical Pharisees

Tradition and custom filled a large place in the so-called "religious" life of the Pharisees. They boasted of superior knowledge and observance of the laws of Moses, according to their own interpretations, which were known as the oral laws of that day. They were called the "separated people," and were known to burn the proverbial midnight oil, studying the musty ancient scrolls and documents containing the early Jewish laws.

Therefore, they claimed to be the sole custodians of the oral laws and traditions, and demanded strict compliance of them, claiming the origin with Moses on Mount Sinai.

The Pharisees taught that fasting for long seasons, with mournful countenances, was most pleasing in the sight of God. With them it was a great sacrilege to partake of a single meal without having first washed his hands to the elbows;[43] and they never failed to condemn any person who ignored their traditions.

There has never been a more egotistical and thoroughly

41) See John 11.
42) Matthew 21:12-13; Mark 11:15-17; Luke 19:45-46; John 2:14-17
43) See Matthew 15:2 and Mark 7:1-4.

hypocritical group. They were haughty, narrow-minded, overbearing, self-satisfied, and strong in the belief that they alone were infallible, impeccable, and better than all the rest, including Christ.

One could easily recognize them anywhere, for they invariably wore the loudest colored, flowing robes with enormous hems, to attract others by their presence. Loud and long were their prayers in public places, as they sought to impress the bystanders with their pretended righteousness and piety.

They were quick to sharply condemn all who failed to do the things which they preached and taught, but did not themselves practice. Their list contained a limited number of things which one *must do*, but set forth hundreds of acts which they *condemned* as unlawful, and contrary to tradition and custom.

This explains their persistence in regarding Jesus, with His message of brotherly love and eternal salvation, as an enemy of their society and their school of thought. Their malice toward Jesus came primarily because He brushed aside the countless absurd traditional practices to which they clung with unswerving devotion.

The Pharisees were ever-ready to embarrass the Master, if they could, by seeking to entrap Him with questions they never dreamed He could answer.

But their pusillanimous[44] conduct and patient hypocrisy was well known to Jesus, for He could read their

---

44) Cowardly and mean-spirited.

minds. They did not fool Him with their repeated acts of piety and pretended reverence for Godly things. So keen was His knowledge of their perfidy[45] that He once said of them in their presence:

> The scribes and the Pharisees sit in Moses' seat: All therefore whatsoever they bid you observe, that observe and do; but do not ye after their works: for they say, and do not.[46]

Jesus never wasted time arguing with them concerning the superficial matter of how thoroughly one should wash his hands and arms before eating, for such was not remotely related to what He taught them to observe and practice.

Jesus made no effort to restrain Himself as He pointed out the absurdity of their devotion to old customs and traditions. Once He told them:

> Thus have ye made the commandment of God of none effect by your tradition… teaching for doctrines the commandments of men.[47]

In other words, the Master said they thought more of their traditions than of the commandments of God; and instead of teaching that one should obey God's commandments, they taught that their substituted commandments, based on those traditions, were superior. With Jesus, it was a matter of which is more important: *human* traditions and customs, or the commandments of *God*.

Knowing the shallowness of their false teachings, and

---

45) Intentional violation of trust; treachery or betrayal.
46) Matthew 23:2-3.
47) Matthew 15:6,9.

that their pitiful efforts at leadership were without any real substance, He said:

> Let them alone: they be blind leaders of the
> blind. And if the blind lead the blind, both
> shall fall into the ditch. [48]

What a spectacle! The blind leading the blind, until both fell into a ditch. Indeed, the Lord exposed them to their ignorant followers. Here is another pointed observation Jesus made about their conduct:

> But all their works they do for to be seen of
> men: they make broad their phylacteries,
> and enlarge the borders of their garments,
> And love the uppermost rooms at feasts, and
> the chief seats in the synagogues, And greet-
> ings in the markets, and to be called of men,
> Rabbi, Rabbi. [49]

Listen to this courageous tongue-lashing from the Lord as He points the finger of guilt at those Pharisees:

> Woe unto you, scribes and Pharisees, hypo-
> crites! for ye devour widows' houses, and for
> a pretence make long prayer: therefore ye
> shall receive the greater damnation.

> Woe unto you, ye blind guides, which say,
> Whosoever shall swear by the temple, it is
> nothing; but whosoever shall swear by the
> gold of the temple, he is a debtor!

---

48) Matthew 15:14.
49) Matthew 23:5-7.

Ye blind guides, which strain at a gnat, and swallow a camel.

Even so ye also outwardly appear righteous unto men, but within ye are full of hypocrisy and iniquity.

Ye serpents, ye generation of vipers, how can ye escape the damnation of hell? [50]

Before Jesus, no one had dared to call the hands of the Pharisees and show them up in public for what they really were. With the Master there was no compromise with false piety, hypocrisy or sin. He exposed it wherever He found it. The better-than-thou Pharisees were no exception.

The condemnation of the Pharisees by Jesus came as a result of them asking Him many questions, hoping that His answers would enable them to lodge and sustain a criminal charge in the Jewish courts, and thus terminate His great ministry.

Were the Pharisees in good faith when they sought to entrap Him into stating that it was unlawful to continue paying tribute money to Caesar? Certainly not. They hoped that a charge of sedition could be lodged against Him as a result of their inquiries.

Let us turn to the New Testament and see what took place concerning the paying of tribute to the Roman Emperor:

Then went the Pharisees, and took counsel how they might entangle him in his talk. And

---

50) Matthew 23:14, 16, 24, 28, 33.

> they sent out unto him their disciples with
> the Herodians, saying, Master, we know that
> thou art true, and teachest the way of God
> in truth, neither carest thou for any man: for
> thou regardest not the person of men. Tell us
> therefore, What thinkest thou? Is it lawful to
> give tribute unto Caesar, or not?[51]

Listen to those hypocrites calling Christ their "Master" and telling Him they know He teaches the way of God in truth. They were trying to play to egotism with their bare-faced lies.

If Jesus had replied that it was not lawful or necessary to pay tribute to Caesar (even though a vast majority of the Jews secretly felt it was unfair and unjust), they would have charged Him with preaching a doctrine contrary to the Roman government's laws.

And they would have been able to destroy Him by proving that He was blocking the Roman's efforts to collect their burdensome taxes from the Hebrews.

But the Lord was too smart for them. He knew that they were not sincere in their inquiry. Perceiving their wickedness and lack of good faith, He replied:

> Why tempt ye me, ye hypocrites? Shew me
> the tribute money.[52]

Ignoring the charge that they were "hypocrites," one of the motley crew quickly handed Jesus a penny:

---

51) Matthew 22:15-17.
52) Matthew 22:18-19.

> And he saith unto them, Whose is this image and superscription? They say unto him, Caesar's. [53]

Jesus answered them in such a manner that they could find no offense:

> Render therefore unto Caesar the things which are Caesar's; and unto God the things that are God's. [54]

When they heard those words, they marvelled and left Him. Another failed attempt to trap Jesus.

Having truthfully accused the Pharisees of being hypocrites, a generation of vipers, robbers of widows' homes, blind leaders of the blind, men who strain at a gnat and swallow a camel, men who for a pretense make long prayer and wear loud-colored garments to be seen of men, and serpents who cannot escape the damnation of hell[55]—they readily co-operated with others who hated Christ, to the end that He might be soon destroyed.

From Love to Hate

Until one understands the great turmoil which permeated Judea during the most critical hours of the earthly life of Jesus, it is hard to understand that on Palm Sunday the streets of Jerusalem were lined with multitudes proclaiming, *"Blessed is he that cometh in the name of the Lord."*[56]

---

53) Matthew 22:20-21.
54) Matthew 22:21.
55) See Matthew 23.
56) See Matthew 21:9, 15; Mark 11:9-10; Luke 19:38 & John 12:13.

The following week those same voices filled the same streets with hatred, shouting *"Let him be crucified."*[57]

Why, in a few fleeting hours, did this throng permit hatred to take the place of love?—because those who hated Jesus had conspired to bring it about.

Those delirious shouts of acclamation for the Master convinced those who hated Christ that unless He was stopped, before long the whole world would be following Him, and the Pharisees and Sadducees, with their narrow versions of shallow, superficial creeds, would fade into the catacombs of oblivion.

Thus we find that Caiaphas and his father-in-law, Annas, completed the deal with Judas Iscariot to betray his friend, the Lowly Nazarene. Then they incited the people to the fact that Jesus did not come to establish an earthly kingdom. Therefore they were following the wrong course if their dreams of an earthly king were to materialize. So they left the Master all alone.

The Unholy Mob

Let us now glance at the unruly, unholy mob as they gloat over their captive Prisoner on the road leading up Calvary's hill.

There was Annas, the disreputable, political boss of Judea, leaning heavily upon the arm of his corrupt son-in-law, the high priest, Caiaphas. Those two were leading the frenzied multitude to the place designated for the cruel crucifixion.

---

57) See Matthew 27:22-23; Mark 15:13-14; Luke 23:21-23; John 19:6, 15.

Immediately behind, we see the cowardly members of the discredited Sanhedrin, chatting amid the smiles of the Sadducees and Pharisees; ignoring the groans of the Saviour as He tries in vain to shift the heavy burden of the cross to another position on His bleeding shoulder.

Yes, they were finally headed toward Golgotha—a place of the skull—and a place hallowed by the fact nowhere else can one find a more convincing proof of Divine love for a lost world, and humble devotion to a Father's will. Other places are more beautiful—but none as sacred.

Oh, what a motley crowd it was which made up the multitude. There were Jews of every age; priests, scribes and Levites; the heartless Roman soldiers being led by the coward, Pontius Pilate, the man who claimed to have washed his hands of the innocent blood.

Following closely behind, we see a few of His friends, their faces filled with grief and fear. Then, with greater courage, but broken hearts, we see the disciple, John, with his arms about the shoulders of the mother of Jesus, as he tries to console that grief-stricken woman, whose eyes are filled with tears.

After Jesus falters because of the great weight of His burden, along comes Simon, who was probably a black man. He leans down and helps the prostrate Christ back to His feet and clutches a portion of the heavy cross to help lighten the awful weight which pressed against the bleeding body of Jesus. This was done without a halt, so the procession of evil men might continue their steady march to the place of murder.

As the crest of Calvary is reached, the Roman soldiers, under the directions of Annas and Caiaphas, begin the nailing of His hands and feet to the cross, as it is lying flat on the ground. Then, with their brute strength, He is lifted into an upright position between the two thieves.

But there was one character missing from the unholy scene—Judas Iscariot. He did not see the culmination of his treachery because by now he was dead and buried in the potter's field, purchased by the high priests with the same filthy silver which was used to effect the betrayal.

Officially, the crowd did not actively participate in the trial or the subsequent crucifixion, but by their presence they became the thoughtless puppets of those unscrupulous leaders, Annas, Caiaphas, and Pilate, and therefore they shared the guilt of what had happened.

To say the least, they rendered a disservice to Christianity and helped place a blot of shame and disgrace upon the sordid names of those who did take active parts.

Also, they willingly joined their voices with the mighty crowd who demanded the release of Barabbas, a confessed murderer, instead of the sinless Christ. Blinded and inflamed by the dire echoes of their own voices, they found themselves clamoring for the innocent blood of Him who had done no wrong.

Then came the consciousness of wrongdoing, for many were heard to say, *"His blood be on us, and on our children."*[58]

While they might have thought they were victorious by

---

58) Matthew 27:25

the enactment of that drama at Calvary, they later learned, with deep regrets, that they had gone through the darkest and most dismal hours of their lives. Because the real and permanent victory was won by the Victim of their vile deeds—Jesus Christ, the Son of the Living God.

This needs to be added to the picture:

There was darkness over the land for three long hours. Immediately after the dying Christ announced *"It is finished"*[59] and commended His Spirit into the hands of His Heavenly Father, His Father took charge. He caused the veil of the temple to be rent in twain from the top to the bottom, and made the earth around them quake and the rocks to be rent. Then one of the evil men of the mob, a Roman soldier, filled with horror and trembling, spoke for all present, saying, *"Truly this was the Son of God."*[60]

---

59) John 19:30.
60) See Matthew 27:54 & Mark 15:39.

CHAPTER 5

NEW TESTAMENT DETAILS OF EVENTS

Let us now copy the New Testament account of what took place from the time of the arrest of Jesus until Pilate released Him to the mob to be crucified:

> ...he went forth with his disciples over the brook Cedron, where was a garden, into the which he entered, and his disciples. And Judas also, which betrayed him, knew the place: for Jesus ofttimes resorted thither with his disciples.
>
> Judas then, having received a band of men and officers from the chief priests and Pharisees, cometh thither with lanterns and torches and weapons.
>
> Jesus therefore, knowing all things that should come upon him, went forth, and said unto them, Whom seek ye? They answered him, Jesus of Nazareth. Jesus saith unto them, I am he.
>
> And Judas also, which betrayed him, stood

with them. As soon then as he had said unto them, I am he, they went backward, and fell to the ground. Then asked he them again, Whom seek ye? And they said, Jesus of Nazareth.

Jesus answered, I have told you that I am he: if therefore ye seek me, let these go their way: [61]

Then Simon Peter having a sword drew it, and smote the high priest's servant, and cut off his right ear. The servant's name was Malchus.

Then said Jesus unto Peter, Put up thy sword into the sheath: the cup which my Father hath given me, shall I not drink it?

Then the band and the captain and officers of the Jews took Jesus, and bound him, And led him away to Annas first; for he was father

---

61) John 18:1-8.

in law to Caiaphas, which was the high priest that same year.

Now Caiaphas was he, which gave counsel to the Jews, that it was expedient that one man should die for the people. And Simon Peter followed Jesus, and so did another disciple: that disciple was known unto the high priest, and went in with Jesus into the palace of the high priest.

But Peter stood at the door without. Then went out that other disciple, which was known unto the high priest, and spake unto her that kept the door, and brought in Peter.

Then saith the damsel that kept the door unto Peter, Art not thou also one of this man's disciples? He saith, I am not.

And the servants and officers stood there, who had made a fire of coals; for it was cold: and they warmed themselves: and Peter stood with them, and warmed himself. [62]

...They said therefore unto him, Art not thou also one of his disciples? He denied it, and said, I am not. One of the servants of the high priest, being his kinsman whose ear Peter cut off, saith, Did not I see thee in the garden with him? Peter then denied again: and immediately the cock crew. [63]

And Peter remembered the word of Jesus, which said unto him, Before the cock crow, thou shalt deny me thrice. And he went out, and wept bitterly. [64]

The high priest (Caiaphas) then asked Jesus of his disciples, and of his doctrine. Jesus answered him, I spake openly to the world; I ever taught in the synagogue, and in the temple, whither the Jews always resort; and in secret have I said nothing.

Why askest thou me? ask them which heard me, what I have said unto them: behold, they know what I said. And when he had thus spoken, one of the officers which stood by struck Jesus with the palm of his hand,

62) John 18:10-18.
63) John 18:25-27.
64) Matthew 26:75.

saying, Answerest thou the high priest so?

Jesus answered him, If I have spoken evil, bear witness of the evil: but if well, why smitest thou me? [65]

Now the chief priests, and elders, and all the council, sought false witness against Jesus, to put him to death; But found none: yea, though many false witnesses came, yet found they none.

At the last came two false witnesses, And said, This fellow said, I am able to destroy the temple of God, and to build it in three days.

And the high priest arose, and said unto him, Answerest thou nothing? what is it which these witness against thee? But Jesus held his peace.

And the high priest answered and said unto him, I adjure thee by the living God, that thou tell us whether thou be the Christ, the Son of God.

Jesus saith unto him, Thou hast said: nevertheless I say unto you, Hereafter shall ye see the Son of man sitting on the right hand of power, and coming in the clouds of heaven.

Then the high priest rent his clothes, saying, He hath spoken blasphemy; what fur-

65) John 18:19-23.

ther need have we of witnesses? behold, now ye have heard his blasphemy. What think ye? They answered and said, He is guilty of death.

Then did they spit in his face, and buffeted him; and others smote him with the palms of their hands, Saying, Prophesy unto us, thou Christ, Who is he that smote thee? [66]

And straightway in the morning the chief priests held a consultation with the elders and scribes and the whole council, and bound Jesus, and carried him away, and delivered him to Pilate. [67]

Pilate then went out unto them, and said,

66) Matthew 26:59-68.
67) Mark 15:1.

What accusation bring ye against this man? They answered and said unto him, If he were not a malefactor, we would not have delivered him up unto thee.

Then said Pilate unto them, Take ye him, and judge him according to your law. The Jews therefore said unto him, It is not lawful for us to put any man to death: [68]

And they began to accuse him, saying, We found this fellow perverting the nation, and forbidding to give tribute to Caesar, saying that he himself is Christ a King. [69]

And when he was accused of the chief priests and elders, he answered nothing. Then said Pilate unto him, Hearest thou not how many things they witness against thee?

And he answered him to never a word; insomuch that the governor marvelled greatly. [70]

Then Pilate entered into the judgment hall again, and called Jesus, and said unto him, Art thou the King of the Jews? Jesus answered him, Sayest thou this thing of thyself, or did others tell it thee of me?

Pilate answered, Am I a Jew? Thine own nation and the chief priests have delivered thee unto me: what hast thou done?

68) John 18:29-31.
69) Luke 23:2.
70) Matthew 27:12-14.

Jesus answered, My kingdom is not of this world: if my kingdom were of this world, then would my servants fight, that I should not be delivered to the Jews: but now is my kingdom not from hence.

Pilate therefore said unto him, Art thou a king then? Jesus answered, Thou sayest that I am a king. To this end was I born, and for this cause came I into the world, that I should bear witness unto the truth. Every one that is of the truth heareth my voice.

Pilate saith unto him, What is truth? And when he had said this, he went out again unto the Jews, and saith unto them, I find in him no fault at all. [71]

And they were the more fierce, saying, He stirreth up the people, teaching throughout all Jewry, beginning from Galilee to this place.

When Pilate heard of Galilee, he asked whether the man were a Galilaean. And as soon as he knew that he belonged unto Herod's jurisdiction, he sent him to Herod, who himself also was at Jerusalem at that time.

And when Herod saw Jesus, he was exceeding glad: for he was desirous to see him of a long season, because he had heard many

---

71) John 18:33-38.

things of him; and he hoped to have seen some miracle done by him. Then he questioned with him in many words; but he answered him nothing.

And the chief priests and scribes stood and vehemently accused him. And Herod with his men of war set him at nought, and mocked him, and arrayed him in a gorgeous robe, and sent him again to Pilate.

And the same day Pilate and Herod were made friends together: for before they were at enmity between themselves.

And Pilate, when he had called together the chief priests and the rulers and the people, Said unto them, Ye have brought this man unto me, as one that perverteth the people: and, behold, I, having examined him before you, have found no fault in this man touching those things whereof ye accuse him:

No, nor yet Herod: for I sent you to him; and, lo, nothing worthy of death is done unto him. I will therefore chastise him, and release him. [72]

But the chief priests and elders persuaded the multitude that they should ask Barabbas, and destroy Jesus. [73]

---

72) Luke 23:5-16.
73) Matthew 27:20.

And they cried out all at once, saying, Away with this man, and release unto us Barabbas: [74]

Pilate saith unto them, What shall I do then with Jesus which is called Christ? They all say unto him, Let him be crucified. [75]

When he [Pilate] was set down on the judgment seat, his wife sent unto him, saying, Have thou nothing to do with that just man: for I have suffered many things this day in a dream because of him. [76]

When Pilate saw that he could prevail nothing, but that rather a tumult was made, he took water, and washed his hands before

74) Luke 23:18.
75) Matthew 27:22.
76) Matthew 27:19.

the multitude, saying, I am innocent of the blood of this just person: see ye to it.

Then answered all the people, and said, His blood be on us, and on our children. [77]

Then Pilate therefore took Jesus, and scourged him. And the soldiers platted a crown of thorns, and put it on his head, and they put on him a purple robe, And said, Hail, King of the Jews! and they smote him with their hands.

Pilate therefore went forth again, and saith unto them, Behold, I bring him forth to you, that ye may know that I find no fault in him.

Then came Jesus forth, wearing the crown of thorns, and the purple robe. And Pilate saith unto them, Behold the man!

When the chief priests therefore and officers saw him, they cried out, saying, Crucify him, crucify him.

Pilate saith unto them, Take ye him, and crucify him: for I find no fault in him. The Jews answered him, We have a law, and by our law he ought to die, because he made himself the Son of God.

When Pilate therefore heard that saying, he was the more afraid; And went again into the judgment hall, and saith unto Jesus, Whence art thou? But Jesus gave him no answer.

---

77) Matthew 27:24-25.

Then saith Pilate unto him, Speakest thou not unto me? knowest thou not that I have power to crucify thee, and have power to release thee?

Jesus answered, Thou couldest have no power at all against me, except it were given thee from above: therefore he that delivered me unto thee hath the greater sin.

And from thenceforth Pilate sought to release him: but the Jews cried out, saying, If thou let this man go, thou art not Caesar's friend: whosoever maketh himself a king speaketh against Caesar.

When Pilate therefore heard that saying, he brought Jesus forth, and sat down in the judgment seat in a place that is called the Pavement, but in the Hebrew, Gabbatha.

And it was the preparation of the passover, and about the sixth hour: and he saith unto the Jews, Behold your King! But they cried out, Away with him, away with him, crucify him.

Pilate saith unto them, Shall I crucify your King? The chief priests answered, We have no king but Caesar. Then delivered he him therefore unto them to be crucified. And they took Jesus, and led him away. [78]

---

78) John 19:1-16.

And he released unto them him that for sedition and murder was cast into prison, whom they had desired; but he delivered Jesus to their will.[79]

The above record of events, now more than two thousand years old, has stood the test of time and criticism. No one, however brilliant, has been able to successfully impeach that testimony. We of the Christian faith have no doubts respecting the authenticity of the account so faithfully recorded by the historian Luke and those eye witnesses, Matthew, Mark and John.

---

79) Luke 23:25.

CHAPTER 6

THE UNLAWFUL ACTS

In the following chapters, we will consider each of the following unlawful acts which were illegally committed against Christ:

1. The arrest was without authority of law, and therefore illegal.

2. Annas, before whom Jesus was first taken for examination, was a mere politician without jurisdiction.

3. The Sanhedrin was unlawfully assembled because Hebrew laws prohibited such a meeting at night, or during the Feast of the Passover.

4. Jesus was first accused of blasphemy, but when He was before Pilate, the charge was changed to sedition, without notice to the Prisoner, or anyone.

5. Jesus was denied an opportunity to obtain His witnesses, who would have testified on His behalf.

6. No person could be found guilty upon his own confession of guilt alone.

7. *At least two witnesses* were required to testify in support of a charge against the accused; and their testimony had to agree as to all the material facts involved.

8. It was not lawful to conclude the trial in a single day.

9. The Roman conquerors had long before taken from the Sanhedrin its authority to sentence anyone to death.

10. A unanimous verdict of guilty rendered on the same day by the Jewish court had the effect of an acquittal.

11. The members of the Sanhedrin were *disqualified* to try Jesus because of enmity toward the accused.

12. The Sanhedrin ignored the merits of Jesus' defense.

13. Pilate, having stated four times that Jesus was not guilty of any wrong, should have released Him instead of delivering Him to the mob for crucifixion.

14. The condemnation of Christ, resulting in His death, was permitted without a lawful judgment of conviction.

15. The Sanhedrin, though learned in the law, ignored every existing Hebrew law that protected the innocent.

Broken Law I

NO AUTHORITY
FOR ARREST

Then the band and the captain and officers
of the Jews took Jesus, and bound him. [80]

Jesus had just left the garden of Gethsemane at the foot
of the Mount of Olives near Jerusalem shortly after midnight when His arrest was effected. ***They had no warrant,***

---

80) John 18:12.

nor authority of arrest whatsoever. The seizing of Christ
was not done, as was customary, by two or three represen-
tatives of justice. Matthew tells us:

> …Judas, one of the twelve, came, and with
> him a great multitude with swords and
> staves, from the chief priests and elders of
> the people. [81]

The "great multitude" consisted of a large group of
Roman soldiers with their drawn swords and staves, plus
several hundred members of the Levitical police, as well
as members of the Sanhedrin, carrying lanterns and torches—confirming that the arrest was made at night.

They evidently thought they might have to search for
Jesus among the orchards of the Garden of Gethsemane,
where Judas had told them He probably would be found,
in prayer to His Heavenly Father.

Little did it matter to the arch traitor that he was guiding the crowd to the hallowed sanctuary of the Son of God.
Nor was he the least concerned over his profaning the Passover, which was the Jew's most sacred Season of the year.
Judas had to earn his fee—had to seal the cheap bargain
which he had made—in order to retain the filthy pieces of
silver. Apparently, nothing else mattered to him.

Why the large group of soldiers, the captain, officers
and others, with drawn swords and staves? Were they ex-
pecting to engage in battle? Or did they think that Christ
would resist their efforts and flee?

---

81) Matthew 26:47.

After having made the arrest, they did not even tell Christ **why He had been apprehended**. This was because there had not been proffered **any charge against Jesus before the Jewish court**.

A warrant, or a written authority, was required before making a lawful arrest. When Saul of Tarsus was on his way to Damascus to arrest any Christians he might find, that he might persecute them, he had to first get his authority for their arrest from the high priest:

> And Saul, yet breathing out threatenings and slaughter against the disciples of the Lord, went unto the high priest, And desired of him letters to Damascus to the synagogues, that if he found any of this way (followers of Christ), whether they were men or women, he might bring them bound unto Jerusalem. [82]

We note this again in Scripture:

> ...I went to Damascus with authority and commission from the chief priests, [83]

Before Saul could arrest those early Christians, he had to obtain the *"authority and commission"* from the high priest.

Why then was no authority for the arrest of Jesus issued by the high priest? Simply because none could be lawfully issued until a criminal charge had been made before the Sanhedrin.

Had Christ been seen committing a crime, the arrest

---

82) Acts 9:1-2.
83) Acts 26:12.

could have been made without a warrant, but He was certainly no law-violator. He was merely leaving the Garden of Gethsemane when the Roman soldiers took Him and bound Him like a common criminal.

Jesus was not surprised by his apprehension. Several days before, He had prophesied to His disciples that they would leave Him all alone at the time of His arrest. So instead of resisting, Jesus quietly said to His disciples:

> …behold, the hour is at hand, and the Son
> of man is betrayed into the hands of sinners. [84]

Then, like the brave Character He was, we see Him standing erect, His countenance aglow in the moonlight as He asked: *"Whom seek ye?"*[85] When they replied, "Jesus of Nazareth," He said, *"I am he."*[86]

As Jesus identified Himself, everyone fell to the ground. After a moment, regaining composure, they arose and Jesus once more asked them the same question: *"Whom seek ye?"* They said: *"Jesus of Nazareth."* Then the Master said:

> I have told you that I am he: if therefore ye
> seek me, let these go their way; [87]

Being unafraid, Christ was willing to bear His cross alone. Hence He requested that His disciples *not* be apprehended. What happened to those disciples? *"And they all forsook him, and fled."*[88]

---

84) Matthew 26:45.
85) John 18:4.
86) See John 18:5.
87) See John 18:7-8.
88) Mark 14:50.

As we get a mental picture of the hasty flight of those eleven disciples—the men who had been so intimately associated with Jesus for the three years of His ministry—we are reminded of a present-day truth: crowds will follow, like blind men, their hero in his days of great triumph, but will leave him at the first sign of adversity.

If these men had intended to conduct a legal trial, a specific charge would have been made against Christ, and a warrant for His arrest would have been issued.

But it was more of a capture than an arrest. They seized Him for the sole purpose of doing away with Him. It was the beginning of a dastardly scheme, born of a cowardly conspiracy, entered into by corrupt and evil men.

Indeed, the condemnation of Christ was agreed to long before His apprehension by the mob. Therefore, the illegal arrest was the least of the many sins committed by those who were referred to by Jesus as "sinful men." Truly He placed them in the right category.

CHAPTER 8

Broken Law II

ANNAS HAD NO JURISDICTION

Having taken Christ into custody, they took Him to Annas, who was the dominating influence over both the Sadducees and the Sanhedrin—where his son-in-law, Caiaphas, was the presiding judge.

He was taken there so Annas might have personal knowledge of His arrest, so he could then contact Caiaphas and have him call a quick nighttime session of a select group of the Sanhedrin, while the friends of Jesus were still asleep.

The private examination of Jesus by old man Annas was illegal for three reasons:

1. It was conducted *at night*, violating Hebrew laws.

2. *No individual*, not even a judge, had the right to question the accused judicially.

3. *Private examinations* of anyone charged with crime were not permitted by the Hebrew law.

Here is an applicable quote from the Jewish law:

> An accused man shall never be subjected to private or secret examination, lest, in his perplexity, he furnish testimony against himself.
>
> Annas, who, with his son-in-law and five sons, had served in the office of high priest for about fifty years, was certainly familiar with this law, which had been in force for over two hundred years. But in his desperation to be rid of Christ, he trampled upon the law in the hope of obtaining an incriminating statement from the lips of Jesus, and thereby have some basis for the filing of criminal charges. Knowledge of the law, followed by a deliberate breach of it, is the best evidence of a willful disregard for the law.

No judge, sitting alone, could conduct an examination of the accused. The lowest Hebrew court was known as the Court of Three, consisting of three judges who sat as a group. Moreover, we know that Annas was not a judge, but a former high priest with no authority.

The above was a good law for the protection of anyone against whom a criminal charge was filed. It protected him from making an incriminating statement which could be used against him at trial.

When Annas had Jesus before him, he inquired as to His disciples and His doctrine. Jesus answered and said:

> I spake openly to the world; I ever taught in the synagogue, and in the temple, whither the Jews always resort; and in secret have I said nothing. Why askest thou me? ask them which heard me, what I have said unto them: behold, they know what I said. [89]

Jesus was well within his legal rights to make such a reply. In effect He was calling attention to the fact that all His teachings were made public, which many had heard.

It was then that one of the petty officers violated the Hebrew law by striking Christ in the face. This corrupt, political boss merely smiled in approval at such unlawful conduct. Jesus made this pertinent remark:

> If I have spoken evil, bear witness of the evil: but if well, why smitest thou me? [90]

---

89) John 18:20-21.
90) John 18:23.

This was a perfect illustration of courage, as well as logic and truth.

Biblical history reveals that Annas, Caiaphas, Pilate and Herod all lived a short distance from each other. Hence, they were in close contact with the situation with a minimum of effort and time. And the time element was to be a factor since they were in a great hurry to have Jesus condemned before His friends became aware of His plight.

Annas knew that whatever the nature of the Kingdom Jesus was advocating, there would be no position therein for him or his colleagues. Kings do not mix with swine.

Not being able to obtain any incriminating statement from Jesus at that secret after-midnight examination, Annas directed the group of men to take Christ before Caiaphas for trial. Far from being a trusting individual, he personally led them to the palace of the high priest.

Moreover, he remained there at the palace of his son-in-law, giving directions and orders as to the proceedings before the Greater Sanhedrin. Annas was not going to miss an opportunity to supervise these cowardly "trials."

Annas had only been before the selected group of the Sanhedrin for a few moments when he began a whispered conference with Caiaphas. "Was the stage all set?" "Had any details been overlooked?" "Were *only* those who opposed Jesus summoned?"

He demanded an affirmative answer to each inquiry. And he was not disappointed with any answers which fell upon his obnoxious ears.

Yes, everyone was ready—even Christ—although He was all alone, friendless, but unafraid.

Caiaphas, in considering the plight of Jesus, said, *"It is expedient for us, that one man should die for the people,"*[91] He thus conveyed that it was thought best to take the life of Jesus for the sake of the people he represented.

It was ironic that Jesus, in quite a different and more reverent sense, likewise felt it was *"expedient that one man should die for the people."*[92] He would be that Man: ready to die for a sin-cursed world, whose only redemption could be found in the precious blood of a crucified Christ.

---

91) John 11:50.
92) John 18:14.

CHAPTER 9

BROKEN LAW III

THE SANHEDRIN'S UNLAWFUL ASSEMBLY

The Hebrew laws were very strict concerning the time during which a case involving the penalty of death could be lawfully tried. [93] In no event could it be held:

1. On a day before the Sabbath.

---

93) See Appendix A for a discussion of the Laws of the Sanhedrin regarding death penalty cases.

2. During the Feast of the Passover, or any festival day. [94]

They shall not judge on the eve of the Sabbath, nor on that of any festival.

3. Never at night.

Let a capital offense be tried during the day, but suspended at night.

When the Sanhedrin assembled that court to try Jesus Christ, they broke all three laws.

It is beyond dispute that Jesus was arrested shortly after the midnight hour as He was leaving the Garden of Gethsemane; and that He was first taken before Annas. His trial before the Sanhedrin began about an hour later, sometime near two o'clock in the morning.

In anticipation of the Great Feast, Jesus had, the night before, partaken of the "last supper" with His disciples in the upper chamber near Jerusalem.

The Jews prohibited the trial of a capital offense at night because:

> "…as oral tradition says, the examination of such a charge is like the diagnosing of a wound—in either case a more thorough and searching examination can be made by daylight."

However, there is another reason. The Jewish religious leaders were obsessed with justifying everything they did

---

94) When you think of Jewish festival days, remember two things: 1) that each day actually began at sunset on the day before; and 2) some of the days of festivals were also treated as "Sabbath days," such as "Firstfruits" during the seven day Feast of Unleavened Bread following Passover.

by the scriptures, no matter how shaky the connection. The rabbis argued this way: In Numbers 25:4 Moses had the idolaters executed "before the Lord against the sun." Therefore, they decided, all decisions in a death penalty case must be decided during the daylight of the second day of the trial. [95]

One might naturally inquire: "Why did the Sanhedrin, in violation of the laws, conduct the sessions at night?"

Those evil-minded cowards were afraid to try Christ in the daytime. They knew that hundreds of His friends were already assembled in Jerusalem to celebrate the great Feast of the Passover. Also, among His many friends were Joseph of Arimathaea and Nicodemus—both members of the Sanhedrin, and men of wide influence.

Those two staunch friends of the Master were known as secret disciples of Jesus and they would have intervened in His behalf. Knowing this, Annas and Caiaphas purposely left them off the list of the members of the Sanhedrin who were summoned to the so-called "trial" of Jesus.

It was Nicodemus who came to Jesus after dark, seeking to learn more of the plan of salvation and eternal life. He undoubtedly looked upon Jesus as the Son of God, for he went to no other in search of the answer to that longing of his soul.

And Joseph of Arimathaea was the rich man who obtained permission from Pilate to bury the body of Jesus in his own personal tomb.

---

95) See the Babylonian Talmud, Bavli Sanhedrin, Chapter 4:1b, (Folios 32A-39B), section IX.1.

The Jews had been taught to never question any act of their high priest. He, like the kings of old, was supposedly incapable of doing wrong.

But how do you suppose they felt down in their hearts on that eve of their Sabbath, and on the great festival day of the Passover, when they witnessed the procession following Jesus to His crucifixion— in full knowledge that their sacred laws were being ruthlessly violated by men whose sworn duty was to uphold them?

This is an example of the powerful influence Annas, Caiaphas and Pilate had on the masses of the Jewish society. Already they had broken *five separate laws*: the unlawful arrest; the unlawful examination by Annas; holding the session at night; on the eve of the Sabbath, and during the Passover. And virtually every act which followed was likewise in deliberate disregard for the Jewish statutes.

When Judas Iscariot made his bargain with Annas and Caiaphas to betray Jesus, it was a part of the unholy conspiracy for Judas to put Christ into their custody while Jesus' friends were unaware of His plight. Judas *"sought opportunity to betray him unto them in the absence of the multitude."*[96]

Those vile conspirators were rightly afraid of the multitudes who were avid followers of Christ—until He was left friendless after His condemnation by the Sanhedrin.

It was Caiaphas who *"sought how they might take him by craft, and put him to death."*[97] Dictionaries define the word

96) Luke 22:6.
97) Mark 14:1.

"craft" as *"deceit, slyness* or *trickery."* They avoided the feast day *"lest there be an uproar of the people."*[98]

What a vile group of law-violators. There they were, supposedly members of a court of justice and impartiality, resorting to deceit to take a human life, under the guise of legal procedure.

No wonder they were apprehensive about the people's reaction. No wonder they did their vile deeds while the moon was hidden behind the clouds. Typical conduct of cowardly men.

---

98) Mark 14:2; see also Matthew 26:5.

CHAPTER 10

Broken Law IV

CHANGING THE FALSE ACCUSATIONS

When Jesus was forcibly hailed before the Sanhedrin, Caiaphas called upon the false witnesses to make their accusations. Then:

> ...came two false witnesses, And said, This
> fellow said, I am able to destroy the temple
> of God, and build it in three days. [99]

Christ never made such a statement. Here are His exact
words on that subject, as related by John:

> Destroy this temple, and in three days I will
> raise it up. [100]

Those two characters purposely perverted the *true* language of Jesus to make it appear that He had threatened
to do physical violence to the Temple of God. Such might
be expected from those whom the high priest himself had
denominated as false witnesses.

Jesus was, of course, referring to His own body as the
"temple" which they had boasted of soon destroying. He
was merely saying that He would raise His body in three
days. John gives the same explanation: *"he spake of the temple of his body."*[101]

Regardless of their efforts to distort the words of
Christ, the two witnesses did not agree concerning what
each claimed to have heard Jesus say. So their testimony
broke down and the false charges had to be abandoned.

Until this time Jesus had not spoken a single word.
Even the hot-headed raging of the high priest failed to extract a single expression from the mouth of their Prisoner.
They were filled with consternation. How, they reasoned,
could they make Him talk?

---

99) Matthew 26:60-61.
100) John 2:19.
101) John 2:21.

Then, like a flash, a clever thought was born in the warped brain of Caiaphas. He rushed from his seat toward Jesus and, in a loud and angry tone, asked, *"Art thou the Christ, the Son of the Blessed?"*[102]

That was the one question Jesus would answer readily, even though it would affirm His Divinity—and His condemnation—and death. Nevertheless, without hesitation, He replied:

> I am: and ye shall see the Son of man sitting on the right hand of power, and coming in the clouds of heaven. [103]

Not only did He tell them He was the Son of the Blessed, but that after his death and resurrection, they would see Him being lifted up in clouds into Heaven, where He would sit at the right hand of His Father.

This greatly intensified the anger of the high priest, and

102) Mark 14:61.
103) Mark 14:62.

he began tearing his robe, while stating to the other members of the Sanhedrin:

> What need we any further witnesses? Ye have
> heard the blasphemy: what think ye? [104]

Being of one accord, they replied: *"He is guilty of death."*[105]

What a trial! What a spectacle in the Jewish court dedicated to the sacred cause of liberty and equality and justice. What indictment could be made against such preposterous outbursts of hatred and cowardly conduct.

We see the presiding officer of the highest court of the Jews personally making the accusation of "blasphemy," and then concluding that the court had no need for witnesses.

What did the members of the court hear? Only the expression of truth—an admission by Jesus Christ that He was the Son of God. And for having spoken the truth, they pronounced, unlawfully, the penalty of death.

Was Christ guilty of blasphemy? An absurd inquiry. Nowhere could there be found any authority to make what Jesus had said the basis for such an accusation.

"Blasphemy" consists of cursing God. We have the benefit of a Biblical definition of that word, as found in the Revelations of John:

> And he opened his mouth in blasphemy
> against God, to blaspheme his name, and his
> tabernacle, and them that dwell in heaven. [106]

---

104) Mark 14:63-64.
105) Matthew 26:66.
106) Revelation 13:6.

The accusation of the high priest was the utterance of a frenzied and prejudiced mind, amounting to nothing more than an illiterate conclusion.[107]

Before the break of day, they took the tired and sleepy Christ to the palace of Pilate, the Roman Governor, to get him to quickly approve the supreme penalty which they had unlawfully imposed upon Jesus. They were hoping for an informal hearing so they might begin their execution.

But the Roman Governor was not only impatient but without affection for the Jews and their numerous religious controversies. He did not wish to be bothered with their bickering and disputing, which he felt they themselves should settle.

As soon as Pilate learned of their presence at the palace, he met them at the entrance gate and said, *"What accusation bring ye against this man?"*[108] They replied with an air of snobbery and presumption:

> If he were not a malefactor, we would not have delivered him up unto thee.[109]

Pilate replied, *"Take ye him, and judge him according to your law."*[110]

Realizing that they could not lawfully condemn one to die by the judgment of the Jewish courts, and doubting that Pilate would approve of their finding Him guilty of blasphemy, they made up an entirely new charge:

---

107) See note on "blasphemy" at the end of this chapter.
108) John 18:29.
109) John 18:30.
110) John 18:31.

> And they began to accuse him, saying, We
> found this fellow perverting the nation, and
> forbidding to give tribute to Caesar, saying
> that he himself is Christ a King. [111]

Jesus remained silent before the Governor of Rome, knowing that the charges of *"perverting the nation, and forbidding to give tribute to Caesar"*[112] were false. Therefore, Pilate marvelled greatly that Christ said not a word.

Then Pilate took Jesus into the judgment hall and asked Him: *"Art thou the King of the Jews?"*[113] Jesus answered:

> Sayest thou this thing of thyself, or did oth-
> ers tell it thee of me? [114]

Jesus continued:

> My kingdom is not of this world: if my king-
> dom were of this world, then would my ser-
> vants fight, that I should not be delivered to
> the Jews: but now is my kingdom not from
> hence. [115]

Pilate became convinced that Jesus had done no wrong, so he brought Him back to the high priest and his followers, and announced, *"I find in him no fault at all."*[116]

That was a verdict of acquittal—a judgment of the Roman Governor, which should have effected the release of Christ.

---

111) Luke 23:2.
112)Luke 23:2.
113) Matthew 27:11; Mark 15:2; Luke 23:3; & John 18:33.
114) John 18:34.
115) John 18:36.
116) John 18:38.

It was the one verdict which fell hard upon the ears of those who hated the Master. Having heard it, they were in a quandary. Then they came to Pilate with a third accusation:

> He stirreth up the people, teaching through-
> out all Jewry, beginning from Galilee to this
> place.[117]

That last charge, while false, was their clever way of telling Pilate that Jesus was from Galilee. Being a Galilean, He would have to be tried before Herod, king of Judea. So Pilate sent Jesus to Herod, who happened to be in Jerusalem at that time.

It was noteworthy that there was a decided departure from the original charge lodged against Jesus before the Sanhedrin, which found Him guilty of "blasphemy."

But when He was brought before Pilate, they changed the charge to "treason," and then to "sedition." Christ was guilty of neither.

Let us note what took place before King Herod:

> And when Herod saw Jesus, he was exceed-
> ing glad: for he was desirous to see him of
> a long season, because he had heard many
> things of him; and he hoped to have seen
> some miracle done by him.[118]

Herod, the murderer of John the Baptist, was still conscious of his wrongdoing, but was unwilling to have his

---

117) Luke 23:5.
118) Luke 23:8.

official acts regarding Christ reported to his political boss, the Emperor of Rome.

So instead of conducting a dignified examination of the complaints made by the Jews, Herod decided to make sport of the Prisoner, hoping to amuse himself and the members of his court.

> Then he questioned with him in many words;
> but he answered him nothing. [119]

Jesus was well acquainted with the character and reputation of this unfit king, Herod, who had shortly before sent a messenger to Christ threatening to have Him killed unless He left the country. But Jesus stood there like a brave soldier and answered him nothing.

That same group stood by, vehemently accusing Jesus before the King. Through it all, the Master maintained a majestic silence. It is highly probable that Jesus, being well versed in the laws of that day, felt that Herod had no right to question Him:

> And Herod with his men of war set him at
> nought, and mocked him, and arrayed him
> in a gorgeous robe, and sent him again to
> Pilate. [120]

Once more we see Christ standing before Pilate. By now Jesus is enveloped in fatigue from loss of sleep and lack of food. Pilate appears irritated. He frankly tells the high priest and the others that they have done a vain thing:

---

119) Luke 23:9.
120) Luke 23:11.

> Ye have brought this man unto me, as one that perverteth the people: and, behold, I, having examined him before you, have found no fault in this man touching those things whereof ye accuse him: No, nor yet Herod: for I sent you to him; and, lo, nothing worthy of death is done unto him. I will therefore chastise him, and release him. [121]

For the second time, Pilate found Jesus guilty of no wrong—and reminded the mob that Herod had done nothing to Jesus. So Pilate said he would chastise Him, then release Him.

But if Jesus was innocent, why should He be "chastised"? It was nothing less than a cowardly subterfuge. Pilate thought that if Jesus were scourged, that would pacify those evil-hearted demons. But they were greatly dissatisfied with Pilate's decision, and showed their anger in no uncertain manner.

Still seeking a way to get from under the burden of the situation, and at the same time hoping to appease the high priest and his followers, Pilate proposed that, since it was the custom during the Passover Feast to release any prisoner they desired, he said to them:

> Whom will ye that I release unto you? Barabbas, or Jesus which is called Christ? For he knew that for envy they had delivered him. [122]

---

121) Luke 23:14-16.
122) Matthew 27:17-18.

Here was Pilate placing the self-confessed murderer beside the sinless Christ, and asking that wild mob which of the two they preferred to be released. Pilate had hopes, though faint, that they might have a change of heart.

But not *that* crowd, for murder filled their hearts, as they remained determined to take the life of Christ. What a compromise to offer—what a proposal to be made by the Roman Governor to a mob of angry Jews.

> But the chief priests and elders persuaded
> the multitude that they should ask Barabbas,
> and destroy Jesus. [123]

Here again we see the scheming Annas with Caiaphas, urging the mob to call for the release of Barabbas. Release Barabbas—so *that they might destroy Jesus.* What a wild scene.

> The governor answered and said unto them,
> Whether of the twain will ye that I release
> unto you? They said, Barabbas. [124]

Pilate, exasperated and impatient, said unto them:

> What shall I do then with Jesus which is
> called Christ? [125]

Why ask such a question? What had Jesus done? Pilate had repeatedly said He was not guilty of any wrongdoing. He should have released Jesus, but he was afraid of that band of Jews, whose continued anger he sought to avoid.

---

123) Matthew 27:20.
124) Matthew 27:21.
125) Matthew 27:22.

"They all say unto him, Let him be crucified."[126] Pilate ignored the plea of his wife to have *"nothing to do with that just man:"*[127]

He called Jesus back into the inner court of the Temple to question Him further, but Jesus remained silent, as before. Then Pilate, for the *third* time, said that he found no wrong in Jesus. Then the Jews cried out: *"Away with him, away with him, crucify him."*[128]

While Pilate sought several times to release Jesus, he did not have the courage of his convictions. He was truly a coward. Then Pilate asked them, *"Shall I crucify your King?"* The mob quickly responded, *"We have no king but Caesar."*[129]

Sensing that Pilate feared them, they hurled the defiant threat toward him:

---

126) Matthew 27:22.
127) Matthew 27:19.
128) John 19:15.
129) John 19:15.

> If thou let this man go, thou art not Caesar's friend: whosoever maketh himself a king speaketh against Caesar. [130]

That did it. Those last remarks placed the pallid flag of fear into Pilate's heart, and he gave in to the demands of evil men. He deliberately ignored all sense of justice and sacrificed his self-respect to quiet the howls of a raging mob:

> Then released he Barabbas unto them: and when he had scourged Jesus, he delivered him to be crucified. Then the soldiers of the governor took Jesus into the common hall, and gathered unto him the whole band of soldiers. And they stripped him, and put on him a scarlet robe. And when they had platted a crown of thorns, they put it upon his head, and a reed in his right hand: and they bowed the knee before him, and mocked him, saying, Hail, King of the Jews! And they spit upon him, and took the reed, and smote him on the head. And after that they had mocked him, they took the robe off from him, and put his own raiment on him, and led him away to crucify him. [131]

Therefore, with no friend willing to speak on His behalf, no friend to protect His legal rights, Jesus was led away by the fiendish mob in preparation for His death on Calvary's cross.

---

130) John 19:12.
131) Matthew 27:26-31.

This final word:

The record reflects that, through it all, the Son of God never made a single murmur or complaint over the many insults heaped upon Him—not even when they crushed the crown of thorns so deeply into His precious brow that His eyes became filled with blood. Yes, He was brave enough to bear it alone in the true spirit of voluntary submission.

He was carrying out the will of His Heavenly Father, and fulfilling the prophecies without complaining of the great pain. The true measure of that pain, which He silently bore for the sins of mankind, is far beyond the pale of human imagination.

Note on the definition of "blasphemy:"

There are 169 instances of forms of the word "blasphemy" in the Talmud. These are the only authoritative ones defining the word, when not in terms of idolatry:

According to Bavli Sanhedrin, Chapter 7:5 (Folios 49B-46A), I.1J, "We require that the Name be cursed by use of the divine Name…" (for the sin of blasphemy to be committed). So, although idolatry can be seen as blasphemy in numerous passages of the Talmud, "the divine Name" – that is, the four-letter name of God – must be used wrongly for the sin of blasphemy to stick to the accused.

In addition, according to 7:5A, "He who blasphemes

[Lev. 24:10] is liable only when he has fully pronounced the divine Name." In fact, Sanhedrin 7:5 is an entire Mishnah-Tractate about this.

The Lord Jesus said, "I am," in answer to the question forced on Him by the high priest:

> Art thou the Christ, the Son of the Blessed?
> And Jesus said, I am: and ye shall see the Son
> of man sitting on the right hand of power,
> and coming in the clouds of heaven. [132]

At the most, the Lord Jesus said, "Ehyeh" – but that isn't even the pronouncing of the full divine Name. In Exodus 3:14 God said "Ehyeh asher ehyeh" (I Am That I Am). When they say "the divine Name," they are referring to the four letters, YHVH, or their pronunciation. But it has to be a curse by the fully-pronounced divine Name in order to be blasphemy and worthy of the death penalty.

---

132) Mark 14:61-62.

CHAPTER 11

Broken Law V

JESUS NOT ALLOWED WITNESSES

After having hurled those false accusations against Jesus, His persecutors ignored His right to a reasonable time to secure His witnesses to refute what had been said, both in the Jewish court and while before Pilate.

Christ could not have had any witnesses present before

the trial began because He was not given any *advance notice* as to what charges they intended to make.

They had no concern for lawful procedure or fairness, for He was not given even a moment to hail before the court a host of friends who would have witnessed for Him.

The initial charge of threatening to destroy the Temple of God was so ridiculous that the prejudiced judges themselves would not act upon such absurd testimony.

Jesus had been teaching and preaching for three years out in the open spaces, as well as within the synagogues and the Temple, before uncounted thousands of men, women and children. His doctrine was well known, for He never taught nor preached in secret.

So there were too many people who knew that Jesus had never threatened to harm God's Temple, but that He was referring to *His Body* and *His resurrection.*

As to the charge that He claimed to be the Son of God and for which He was condemned to die for "Blasphemy," He could have had thousands come forth who had been healed through the miraculous power of God.

Out of that crowd, a number of Jesus' followers would have been eager to affirm His Divinity, people like Lazarus' sister Martha (John 11:27).

They knew well that no mere prophet, nor any other human being, could have done the things which Jesus did. No human could have said the things which Jesus said; or led the perfectly sinless life that Jesus led. Yes, by the thousands, they sincerely believed Him to be what He *was,* and *is* —the Son of the living God.

What about the great horde of people who were the direct beneficiaries of His compassion?:

- Bartimaeus, whose sight was restored.
- The group of paralytics.
- The host of lepers.
- The centurion of Rome, whose servant was healed merely by saying the word.
- The widow whose son was brought back to life.
- Jairus, whose dead daughter was made to live again.
- The hundreds of deaf and dumb, and the halt and the lame, who were healed.
- The poor convulsed child.
- The man who was blind from birth and was made to see.
- The badly crippled woman.
- His good and devoted friend, Lazarus, who was brought back to life *from a four-day-old grave.*
- Many saw the Master walk calmly upon the sea.
- Nine thousand men and women who were miraculously fed with a handful of small fishes and a few loaves of barley bread.

As a climax to such an array of trustworthy witnesses, there would have come Mary and Martha, sisters of Lazarus. Would it not be convincing proof of His Divinity to hear Lazarus describe the sensation, after reposing for four days and nights in a cold and silent grave, to be awakened and released from the throes of death at the majestic command of the Son of God?

Consider the hundreds who were present when Jesus

was baptized by John, and heard the glorious voice of God penetrating from the skies of Heaven, announcing:

.. This is my beloved Son, in whom I am well pleased. [133]

Then call Peter, James and John, the disciples who were present at the Transfiguration, who heard the voice of God repeating the affirmation that Jesus was His Son. [134]

Indeed, Christ would not need any better witnesses than those. They could have readily dispelled any doubt of His identity.

Nicodemus, a member of the Sanhedrin, though absent during the "trial," would have certainly testified that Jesus was the Son of God. He believed it so strongly that he went to Christ at night seeking answers about his own salvation through Jesus.

Joseph of Arimathaea, a noble man—and another absent member of the Sanhedrin—believed sincerely that Jesus was the Son of God. So definite was his belief that, in spite of threats of the Jews, Joseph insisted that Jesus be buried in his personal tomb. It took a man of courage to do that—one who believed that Christ was the Son of God.

Except for the rush to murder Him, Jesus could have had ample witnesses to establish that He spoke only the *truth* when responding to the inquiry of the high priest. But when evil men have murder in their hearts, they give no thought to orderly, legal procedures, or justice.

---

133) Matthew 3:17; see also Mark 1:11 & Luke 3:22.
134) See Matthew 17:5; Mark 9:7; Luke 9:35.

CHAPTER 12

BROKEN LAW VI

NO CONVICTION ON CONFESSION ALONE

As soon as Jesus admitted that He was the Son of God, the proceedings in the Sanhedrin were abruptly halted by Caiaphas who, with his cohorts, adjudged Christ guilty of blasphemy, and condemned Him to death.

Thus, Jesus was convicted and condemned *solely upon His own confession to being the Son of God.* Witnesses were not used upon either side. The Jews felt they needed none, and they denied Jesus His right to obtain any.

I have never heard of any court proceedings that reveal a parallel or precedent for condemning one upon his own confession without supporting witnesses. Where it has happened before, it was *outside of courts,* and in limited and isolated instances, where mob-rule prevailed.

What then in defense of the Jews as a group? Did the Jewish society when Jesus was "tried" approve of such tactics? They most assuredly did not. Let us turn to the solemn pronouncement of the Hebrew laws on that subject:

"We have it as a fundamental principle of our jurisprudence that no one can bring an accusation against himself. Moreover, a voluntary confession on his part is not admitted in evidence, and therefore not competent to convict, unless a legal number of witnesses minutely corroborate his self-accusation."

Note how simple and unambiguous is this statement of Jewish law. In easily-understood language, no one can bring an accusation against himself. If one volunteers a confession, it cannot be considered evidence unless a legal number of witnesses corroborate his self-accusation.

Did they not convict and condemn Jesus upon His voluntary confession that He was the Son of God? And did they require that the legal number of witnesses support the confession? The answers are self-evident.

To the credit of the early Jewish lawmakers of Israel, they did employ many sound legal principles and rules of orderly court procedures, which, if fairly enforced, would have provided sufficient safeguards for the protection of those charged with crime.

The trouble came by the haphazard and too frequently spiteful manner in which they were ignored by judges who had sworn to enforce them.

Had Jesus Christ been given the benefit of existing Hebrew laws, as well as fairness in the enforcement of them, He would never have been subjected to the series of humiliations and acts of brutality which were so wrongfully imposed by corrupt administrators. It was not a matter of being ignorant of the laws because each member of the Sanhedrin was required to be well-versed in the laws of Israel. Spite and hatred moved their hearts against Christ. Nothing else mattered to them.

Too frequently men have made what appeared to be a voluntary confession of a crime which they had not committed in order to "cover up" for some friend or relative.

Then there are instances where an investigation later revealed that a crime for which the accused "confessed" had never been committed. This is always a tragic spectacle.

Having condemned Jesus to die solely upon His *"confession,"* or to use a better word, His *"admission"* that He was Christ, without the required number of witnesses, placed the high priest and the entire Sanhedrin into the category of *law-violators* because they breached the solemn laws on that subject.

The succeeding chapter will discuss the legal number of witnesses which had to be produced by the prosecution before a conviction could be valid.

CHAPTER 13

BROKEN LAW VII

REQUIREMENT FOR TWO WITNESSES

The Hebrew laws, both Mosaic and Talmudic, insisted that *no less than two witnesses* testify against the accused in all criminal cases. Moreover, their testimony had to agree in all essential facts of the charge.

> "At the mouth of two witnesses, or three witnesses, shall he that is worthy of death be put to death; but at the mouth of one witness he shall not be put to death. [135]

By this law, even if they had found only *one witness* to testify against Jesus—which they did not have—He could not have been lawfully condemned to die.

Only eye witnesses were permitted to testify against the prisoner. In those days, there was no such thing as "circumstantial evidence" in a criminal prosecution. Additionally, the testimony of all witnesses had to embrace all of the

---

135) Deuteronomy 17:6.

case—not a part by one, and another part by some other witness. Unless the witnesses could relate the details of the whole crime, their testimony was considered unworthy of belief. This was a rather harsh rule, long since departed from in modern jurisprudence, but it is evidence of a sincere determination on their part to be absolutely fair and impartial in dealing with the accused.

Before taking the stand, every witness was solemnly warned about testifying falsely against his neighbor, in keeping with the law of Moses, embraced in the Ten Commandments, received by him on Mount Sinai.

Thou shalt not bear false witness against thy neighbor. [136]

It is of further interest to note that under the Jewish laws, a witness was not called upon to swear that he would speak only the truth. No oath was required of him, as is now the rule in all courts, because the early Jews concluded that any testimony offered in their courts was submitted

136) Exodus 20:16; see also Deuteronomy 5:20.

under the admonition of God, set forth in the above quoted ninth Commandment.

Not only did the Hebrew laws require the testimony of at least two witnesses, but the competency of such witnesses was very limited. Take, for example, these limitations:

Women, even though eye witnesses to a crime, were never permitted to testify. Notice the peculiar reasons assigned for excluding them:

> Let not the testimony of women be admitted
> in evidence, on account of their levity and
> boldness of their sex.

Such a prohibition against womanhood is unheard of in modern jurisprudence. Almost worldwide they are now seen as competent to serve as judges and jurors. Some of the ablest jurists in America are of the female gender.

Into what common classification were women placed by the early Jewish laws? Besides women, the following were likewise incompetent to testify in any case:

> Slaves, minors, idiots, the blind, deaf mutes,
> usurers, [137] gamblers, illiterates, and anyone
> directly interested in the outcome of a case.

This Jewish "two-witness" rule was long ago abandoned in every jurisdiction, except in a limited scope of crimes, such as perjury and the serious offense of treason.

Another strange provision of ancient Jewish laws — foreign to modern requirements —was that of not requiring the accused or his witnesses to take an oath to tell the

---

137) Those who lend money out for the interest.

truth. This was for three reasons: first, they thought the 9th Commandment, "Thou shalt not bear false witness," would discourage perjury. Second, any witness who did commit perjury in a capital case would be executed himself. And third, if the accused were convicted, the witnesses had to attend the execution.

In modern times, testimony must be taken under oath, including cases where the accused testifies in his own behalf. However, in military tribunals in the United States, members of the armed forces, when tried by court martial, cannot be forced to testify under oath.

Therefore, from the first step to the last stage of the "trials" of Jesus, including His sentence of death, *not a single witness supported the high priest's charge of "blasphemy."* Therefore, under the law, Christ stood acquitted and was entitled to an immediate judgment of *"not guilty."*

Jesus was well versed in the Hebrew laws. More than once, He properly challenged their legal right to treat Him as they did. Had He not been within His legal rights, they could have forced Him to speak when He elected to remain silent. And while they marvelled at His majestic silence, they could not condemn Him for it because He was exercising His legal rights.

Thus, those who nailed Jesus to that cross were no less than murderers because they had no legal mandate so to do from a lawful court. Annas, Caiaphas and the other members of the Sanhedrin were as guilty of that murder of the Innocent Blood as were the Roman soldiers who had the gall to gamble for the garments of the dying Christ.

CHAPTER 14

BROKEN LAW VIII

DEATH TRIAL CAN'T END IN ONE DAY

"A criminal case, where a death sentence is to be pronounced, cannot be concluded before the following day."

Therefore, it was unlawful for the Sanhedrin to conclude the trial of Jesus, with the imposition of the penalty of death, in a single day.

Long before the ministry of Christ, the Hebrew jurists concluded that an *acquittal* of the accused may be accomplished within one day, but not a *conviction*. It was a serious matter to be called upon, in a judicial proceeding, to take human life. It was thought best to give more time for sober reflection and prayer before imposing such a verdict.

The Jewish law-writers, with full approval of the Jewish society, clung to the notion that at least two days should be consumed in the trial of such cases; that the judges should have a good night's rest, and have more time for a full review of the evidence on the following day.

From the best available sources (Matthew, Mark and Luke) it has been established that the "trials" of Jesus — both the Hebrew and Roman — lasted about seven hours and were concluded on the same day. The first was held between one and two o'clock A.M., and the second just about daybreak on the same fateful morning. This is another illustration of them ignoring their own laws.

In every other case, the judges would retire to their homes after the first day of trial and engage in prayer for heavenly guidance, that they might not commit an error while dealing with the life of a human being.

Then, after long searches for possible mistakes in judgment, they would reassemble in the halls of the Sanhedrin and review all that had transpired on the previous day. It was an unforgivable offense against one's conscience as well as the good of the Jewish society for an error to be made. They were honor-bound by their oath of office to diligently safeguard the paramount rights of the accused.

But with Jesus it was different. The air of solemnity and sacredness was missing. The high honor due the judicial robes was overlooked. Instead of permitting their legal minds to ponder justice and impartiality in the discharge of their sacred duty, they could see only a "Culprit" who had dared to overturn the tables of the money-changers in the Temple; and who repudiated their religion, which taught that there was no such thing as the resurrection, by calling Lazarus back to life.

Little did they care that after two thousand years, millions would still discern the echo of their treachery.

But let us note this significant fallacy:

Even if the high priest and his cohorts had retired to the quiet of their homes after the first day, they would have been prohibited by the same Jewish law from returning on the next day, for *that would have been the Sabbath.* Apparently, they were willing to break every existing Jewish statute thus far; but it would not do to vote the verdict of death on their *Sabbath.*

To pacify their insatiable demand for the life of Christ, they rushed the proceedings to a quick and tragic conclusion—typical of after-midnight mob violence.

When vile men have thoughts of murder, born of hate and spite, they no longer entertain conceptions of justice, morals or law. Such were the hearts and minds of those disreputable members of the Sanhedrin who placed a blight and stain upon the name of "justice," and who supplanted *corruption* in the stead of *impartiality.*

Their base deeds of treachery will ever be despised by honorable men and women. As long as God gives mankind the ability to read His Holy Word, they shall find the sordid narration of inhuman brutality imposed upon Christ. Each time they read those accounts, their hearts will boil in bitter resentment over what transpired before the Sanhedrin, Herod and the "court" of Pontius Pilate.

CHAPTER 15

Broken Law IX

SANHEDRIN CAN'T AUTHORIZE DEATH PENALTY

Was it lawful for the Jews, the members of the Sanhedrin, to take the life of Jesus Christ? The answer must be in the negative because ***they had no such authority***.

Judea was a province under the domination of its Roman conquerors. They were denied the power to execute any sentence involving the taking of human life. However, the Romans did permit them to *try* persons accused of offenses for which the death penalty might be imposed; but such a sentence first had to be submitted to the Roman Governor, Pontius Pilate, for his approval.

Moreover, Pilate was required to hear the testimony and weigh the evidence which was heard by the Sanhedrin, and *then* make his decision.

If the Sanhedrin tried a man for a capital offense involving the infliction of the death penalty, and he was found not guilty, then that was the end of the trial. But all convictions were required to be taken before Pilate, whose final decision was necessary before the judgment of the Sanhedrin could be put into effect.

During the trial of Jesus before the Sanhedrin, Caiaphas and his henchmen found Jesus guilty of "blasphemy" and pronounced the sentence of death. But instead of complying with the Hebrew laws, they took Christ before Pilate, not to obtain a review of their decision, but to get a quick approval of their unlawful acts, without telling the Roman Governor why Jesus had been condemned to die.

When appearing before the Roman Governor, they were afraid to report the truth: that Jesus had been found guilty of blasphemy without any testimony, or a single witness. Instead they told Pilate, *"If he were not a malefactor, we would not have delivered him up unto thee."*[138]

Of course, they were hopeful that Pilate would not ask why they had condemned Jesus to die, but they were mistaken. Pilate inquired *"What evil hath he done?"*[139] Apprehensive to tell the truth, fearing that Pilate would ridicule their judgment of condemnation upon such an absurd charge without any evidence, they quickly changed the charge from "blasphemy" to "sedition."

When Pilate told them to *"Take ye him, and judge him according to your law,"*[140] they were confounded. Caiaphas and Annas knew that they had no lawful right to cause the death of Jesus, and they knew that Pilate could not legally

138) John 18:30.
139) Matthew 27:23; Mark 15:14 & Luke 23:22.
140) John 18:31.

permit the Sanhedrin to take the life of Christ without a thorough investigation of the charges against Him.

Still, in their determination to destroy Jesus, they resorted to subterfuge and trickery before Pilate by accusing the Lord of sedition, hoping the Roman Governor would affirm their verdict of the death penalty, even though based on blasphemy.

When they saw that their plot was about to fail, they resorted to pressure tactics, threatening to report the Roman Governor to Caesar as not being a loyal friend of the Emperor. This was the trick which caused Pilate to vacillate and give in to the demands of the mob.

They were able to gain the custody of Christ, but not under sanction of the laws. From the moment Pilate delivered Christ unto them, they began their plans to destroy Him.

"…and led him away to crucify him."[141]

They crucified Him with the full knowledge that their acts were criminal, in that they violated the laws of God and the laws of their race, for neither the Jews nor God sanction cold-blooded murder.

---

141) Matthew 27:31.

CHAPTER 16

BROKEN LAW X

DEATH SENTENCE CAN'T BE UNANIMOUS

The most unusual of all the pronouncements of the ancient Jewish laws was that the verdict of the Sanhedrin could *NOT* be unanimous in death penalty cases.

Modern jurisprudence, extending back a thousand years, has provided, in direct conflict with that odd Hebrew statute, that no man could be sentenced to die until there was a unanimous verdict. If all did not agree, then a mistrial would be entered and the accused would be tried a second time.

Here is that rare, and now long-forgotten law:

> "The unanimous verdict of guilt, in a capital case, has the effect of an acquittal."

Therefore, under the Jewish laws, regardless of how heinous an offense might be, if the death sentence was sought, the accused went free unless the vote was *not* unanimous.

There was another unusual provision. A vote of fifty percent of the Sanhedrin, plus two additional members was required before one could be convicted, but any majority vote for acquittal would result in his freedom. This, however, applied only to the Great Sanhedrin, the court in which Christ was "tried."

Remember, in the time of Christ, lawyers did not defend people charged with crimes. The "lawyers" and scribes were men well versed in the Mosaic laws, and would interpret them for the officers of the courts—but that was the limit of their activities. It was mainly for that reason that the court officers usually performed the duties of modern-day lawyers in the Jewish courts.

Since the accused had no one to defend him, it was the sworn duty of the judges to see that his rights were protected, that he had a fair and impartial trial, that no advantage was taken of him by the court, that a guilty verdict was based on believable and competent testimony beyond a reasonable doubt, and to a moral certainty.

So the judges of the Sanhedrin were obliged to be the defenders of the prisoner. To do otherwise would amount to *mob violence*. And the Sanhedrin certainly did not want mob violence to take over and control the court. *That is, not until Jesus appeared before them.*

In spite of the Hebrew laws quoted above, we come to the question of the Sanhedrin's verdict of guilt. After the high priest rent his clothes, he cried:

> "What need we any further witnesses? Ye have heard the blasphemy: what think ye? And *they all condemned him to be guilty of death.*"[142]

"All" means "everyone" present. So it was unquestionably a unanimous verdict of guilt. **Since it was *unanimous*, it was *in violation of the Jewish law, and void.***

How could one possibly defend those corrupt men by trying to justify their unlawful acts? They obviously knew the laws of their own society, but they ignored them.

Immediately after Caiaphas heard the vote of his fellow judges, under the law of unanimity, he would have had to announce the acquittal of Jesus. That is, if he had followed the law which he was sworn to do.

Instead, with a glow of satisfaction, he accepted it as final and legal, then made plans to take the bound Christ before the Roman Governor for his approval.

---

142) Mark 14:63-64.

Broken Law XI

SANHEDRIN MEMBERS WERE DISQUALIFIED

The Hebrew laws plainly set forth the caliber of men who could serve in the Sanhedrin —the loftiest position in the Jewish society—by requiring certain qualities.

This was to insure that members of this supreme court of Judea would be fair and impartial in their dealings with the accused. Nothing will more quickly degrade the cause of justice than a corrupt, prejudiced jurist.

Certainly it was with this thought in mind that the Hebrew law-promoters, long before the trials of Christ, enumerated the qualifications of their judges, the members of the Sanhedrin.

Irrespective of the heinousness of the crime which one may commit, he is entitled to have his guilt or innocence honestly decided by judges who are free of corruption, prejudice, bias and ill-will. This is of paramount importance to all peoples, regardless of race, religion, creed or color.

When courts try men for their lives or their liberties,

and are solemnly dedicated to those principles, they are irreparably stained when cruel and depraved men occupy those high positions of trust and responsibility.

Remembering, then, the attitudes so patently manifested by the Sanhedrin in its treatment of Christ, it will be interesting to now quote the Hebrew laws setting forth the requirements of those who would serve there:

> "Nor must there be on the judicial bench either a relation, or a particular friend, or an ENEMY of either the accused or the accuser."

> "Nor under any circumstances, was a man known to be at enmity with the accused person permitted to occupy a position among the judges."

To analyze the statute, let us make these observations:

1. The judge could not serve if he were *"an enemy of the accused."*

Without question, Caiaphas considered Christ an enemy. Was it not he who, in a fit of rage, boasted of his plan to *seek false witnesses that he might destroy Jesus, by craft?*[143]

Was it not he who conspired with Annas, his father-in-law, and Judas Iscariot, to betray Him?

Was it not he who stated before Jesus had even been arrested that "It was expedient that one man should die for the people."?[144]

---

143) See Mark 14:1.
144) John 18:14.

Was it not he who, determined to shed the Innocent Blood of Jesus, procured "false witnesses" to condemn Christ?

Who else but Caiaphas preferred the false accusation of "blasphemy," then called for a vote, stating that there was no further need for witnesses?

Who else but he had Jesus taken before Pilate to obtain approval of his scheme to murder the Son of God?

Whose voice was louder than Caiaphas, when the mob cried: *"Away with him, away with him, crucify him?"*[145]

2. The judge must not serve if he be "related to the accuser."

Biblical history reveals that Annas, Caiaphas, and the five sons of Annas all voted for Christ's condemnation.

Were Annas and his son-in-law "related?" And who but Caiaphas made the accusation of "blasphemy?" Was not Annas the "accuser" of Christ? Were not the five sons of Annas related to the accuser, Caiaphas?

Hence, the whole bunch were not only unfit, but utterly disqualified. They each had agreed to condemn and crucify Jesus several days *before* His arrest.

Jesus knew well their hearts and hypocrisy, and thus said to them:

> "Ye serpents, ye generation of vipers, how can ye escape the damnation of hell?"[146]

---

145) John 19:15.
146) Matthew 23:33.

CHAPTER 18

Broken Law XII

CHRIST'S DEFENSE WAS IGNORED

Criminal cases in all courts embrace two divisions:

1. The presenting of a formal charge against the prisoner, setting forth in plain language the nature of the offense with which he has been charged; then the introduction of witnesses to establish guilt, beyond a reasonable doubt.

2. Permitting the accused to plead guilty or not guilty. Where the plea is "not guilty," he is granted reasonable time to prepare his defense. He may then, at trial, introduce his witnesses to corroborate his version of what happened.

Courts are places where both sides of a controversy are heard. They must be conducted in an atmosphere of impartiality with equal justice, so as to be entirely free of secrecy, confusion, conspiracies, distrust and fear. For it is only through the assurance of fairness, impartiality and equality that justice may be ultimately attained.

Moreover, the character or reputation of the accused, or the severity of the crime with which he stands charged,

133

should never be cause to change or deny to him those fundamental rights prescribed by orderly, legal proceedings.

With this brief outline of how courts are supposed to operate, it is difficult to conceive of the fair administration of justice when the accused is deliberately denied his right to establish his defense to the charges made against him.

As we recall those repeated acts of violence which were mercilessly perpetrated by the judges of the highest Jewish court during the trial of Jesus, let us note what the Hebrew Code required of those members of the Sanhedrin:

> "The judges shall weigh the evidence in the sincerity of their conscience."

That was a laudable admonition to the judges to be fair in all their dealings with the accused. Then there was this added injunction in respect to their solemn duties while presiding in that court:

> "Then shalt thou inquire, and make search, and ask diligently."

It is apparent that the ancient Jewish law-writers of Israel desired a court composed of honorable judges who would deal fairly with the accused. The trouble, however, came not from the laws or procedures, but by placing on the court men who were inherently corrupt, biased and cowardly, who deliberately ignored all law while dealing with Jesus Christ.

Could it be said that a single judge of the Sanhedrin ever, during that trial of the Master, gave any evidence of an intent or purpose to *weigh the law and testimony in the sincerity of his conscience?* They not only were devoid of conscience, but lacked every vestige of sincerity when Jesus was before them. Indeed, those immoral, evil men were motivated, not by a sense of justice, but by deep-seated hatred and a determination to murder their helpless Victim —regardless of the means to that sordid end.

Truly, when the putrid poison of hate abounds in the human heart, one is no longer able to think clearly nor to judge honorably and justly —regardless of law and order, rules of legal procedure, or anything else.

To be sure, they can never be successfully defended upon such a false premise that they "did not know better." They were all men who were well-versed in the laws of their own society; and the knowledge of the laws was a strict prerequisite to their appointment upon that Supreme Court of Israel. Had a single one of them not been well trained as to all the laws of his country, he could never have stood the rigid test of legal learning.

But in spite of their full knowledge of the Hebrew laws, and their familiarity with what was expected of them as judges, they busy themselves, days before the trial of Jesus in a contemptible conspiracy to seek "false witnesses." And when their "false witnesses" indicted their souls with corruption by relating bare-faced falsehoods, their testimony was found wholly unworthy of belief.

Finding themselves in this plight, with its attending humiliation and embarrassment, we see the high priest venting his uncontrollable rage by tearing his own robe as he absurdly accused Christ of "blasphemy," with not a single witness to support his deductions.

While Jesus was before the Roman Governor, Pilate, the charge was then changed to "sedition," in that, as they again falsely claimed, *"He stirreth up the people…"*[147] by teaching that it was not lawful to pay tribute to Caesar.

We remember that this charge, like the first, failed miserably because no one was found to testify before Pilate that they had ever heard Jesus make any such statement. It was all right for them to obtain false witnesses to appear before their own court, but when they were before Pilate, they were desperately afraid to assume the role of "false witnesses."

Reverting back to those solemn admonitions to the judges: Where was their memory to *"weigh the evidence in the sincerity of their conscience?"* Where, except for the voluntary admission of Christ that He was the Son of God, was there any *evidence* before the court? And how could they *weigh* that which was not in existence?

Another pertinent inquiry:

How could they get around their solemn duty, under the previously quoted Jewish law, to *"Inquire, make search, and ask diligently?"*

We know, now, that there was no "search" made by any of them. And the only "inquiry" during the Jewish trial, came from the putrid lips of the high priest when he asked Christ if He was the Son of God.

There would be little occasion to now argue that the Sanhedrin would have been forced to acquit Jesus when

147) Luke 23:5.

they had heard His many witnesses; for surely they, with their vicious attitude toward Him, would have ignored them all. But, to say the least, they could have saved themselves much of the justified condemnation to which they have, for nearly two thousand years been subjected, had they given Christ a chance to be supported by His witnesses, so He could have had His day in court.

Had they followed the established rules of court procedure, set forth by their own laws, there would have been *no conviction of Christ for any offense whatsoever*. And His right to interpose a defense of any kind would never have been an issue to be decided then, nor to be debated now —because Christ would have been acquitted because of *the absence of a single witness against Him.*

When Jesus told the Sanhedrin, in response to the inquiry of the high priest, that He was the Son of God, and they immediately adjudged Him to be guilty of "blasphemy," why did they not produce a few more of their "false witnesses" to disprove His claim of being the Messiah?

It follows that if what He had said was not the truth— then He would be guilty of blasphemy. But the burden of proof was on the Sanhedrin, and not Christ. **Neither He, nor any other prisoner, under the Hebrew laws, was ever required to establish His own guilt**. That was the task and responsibility of the Sanhedrin—and they well knew that. In the absence of proof, then, the high priest's fallacious charge of "blasphemy" did not make it such an offense, for the law was definitely to the contrary.

It is not the purpose of the author to spend even a fleeting second in an attempt to create a defense for Christ. He needed no defense then, and He needs none now. That absurd accusation of the high priest was no more than a wild outburst of a prejudiced heart, born in a corrupt mind which had become warped and twisted by a lust for murdering the Lord Jesus.

Without question, the defense of Jesus was ignored. But we are reminded of that true adage:

"Truth crushed to the earth will rise again."

Jesus spoke only the truth, and nothing but the truth but when He spoke it, they took His life on Calvary's cross —but, on the third day, the great stone was rolled away by the handiwork of God and He arose victorious—forever!

CHAPTER 19

Broken Law IX

CHRIST'S CONVICTION WAS UTTERLY VOID

When the mob crucified Jesus, it was solely because they had condemned Him when He was before the Sanhedrin. Did the Sanhedrin act in keeping with the Hebrew laws when they sentenced the Master to die? If they did, then the judgment of conviction would have been lawful; otherwise, it was absolutely void.

A casual review of what transpired should forever settle the validity of the sentence of death. Let the reader consider these salient facts, which cannot be disputed:

1. Jesus was unlawfully arrested because they had no warrant nor authority from the high priest, or anyone else, to take Him into custody. (See Chapter 7.)

2. He was illegally taken before Annas for private examination. Annas was neither a judge or high priest, but a mere politician in Judea. (See Chapter 8.)

3. The members of the Sanhedrin were disqualified to try Jesus because of their known enmity toward the pris-

oner; and because they had prejudged His case long before the trial had begun. (See Chapter 17.)

4. The Sanhedrin had no lawful right to assemble when they did —the night before the celebration of the Feast of the Passover. (See Chapter 9.)

5. The proceedings were void because when the trial started, no charges had been filed.

6. The Sanhedrin violated the Jewish laws by failing to produce the required *two witnesses*. (See Chapter 13.)

7. The Sanhedrin had no jurisdiction because Jesus was brought before them without a warrant of arrest. No court acquires jurisdiction over one's person until he has been subjected to a legal arrest.

8. They failed to produce any witnesses to establish that Christ was not the Son of God. They should have proved, beyond a reasonable doubt, and to a moral certainty, that Jesus lied when He confessed to being the Son of God.

9. The proceedings were void because, without notice to the Accused, the charges were changed. He was first charged with the "blasphemy," then with treason and sedition when before the Roman Governor. (See Chapter 10.)

10. The conviction was illegal in that the entire proceedings against Him were *ex parte*—that is, one-sided, because they would not permit Him to call His witnesses to corroborate Him. (See Chapter 11.)

11. They unlawfully condemned Him to die on His Own admission that He was the Son of God. This was contrary to the Hebrew laws of evidence. (See Chapter 12.)

12. The Sanhedrin, contrary to the law, concluded His trial on the same day, when it was required to last at least two days. (See Chapter 14.)

13. The conviction was void because He was denied His right to set forth His defense to the charges made against Him. (See Chapter 18.)

14. There was a unanimous verdict of guilty, and, under the Hebrew laws, a unanimous verdict amounted to an acquittal of the Accused. (See Chapter 16.)

15. They had no lawful right to take Christ before Herod for trial because there were no charges preferred against Him while He was before King Herod. In spite of this error, Herod did *not* condemn Jesus for any crime.

16. Christ was unlawfully condemned to die because the Sanhedrin had no lawful right to condemn anyone to death unless that sentence was approved by the Roman Governor.

17. The Hebrew laws operated to acquit Christ when He was before the Sanhedrin. He should have been released instead of being taken before Pilate. Having proved nothing, the Sanhedrin unlawfully took Him before the Roman Governor for the approval of their unlawful conduct.

18. Pilate tried four times to release Jesus by declaring that he did not find Him guilty of any offense. In spite of this, they murdered Him upon Calvary.

These eighteen serious law-violations were spitefully committed by that group of evil-minded men who, in order to be rid of Jesus, were willing to stoop to murder.

CHAPTER 20

SHADOWS OF THE CROSS WERE FAST FALLING

Jesus left the carpenter shop of His foster father, Joseph, in the little village of Nazareth in AD 27 to engage in His ministry, which took Him into every sector of Israel, teaching and preaching, in search of lost men and women, that He might show them the plan for eternal life.

In carrying out the will of His Heavenly Father He soon met with violent opposition from the Sadducees and Pharisees because of the wide difference in what each taught and believed.

The Jews at that time were wedded to the Mosaic Code which, among other things, asserted the philosophy that in retaliation one should have an eye for an eye and a tooth for a tooth. But Jesus sought to change such a belief by teaching that one should love his neighbor as himself—that a man should forgive his brother, not seven times seven, but seventy times seven.

Also, we should only do to others that which we would have them do to us. He healed the lame, restored sight to the blind, and more than once brought the dead back to life. Those miracles brought to Him thousands of follow-ers who willingly deserted the Sadducees and Pharisees to enjoy the thrill of companionship with Christ.

More than once, they virtually demanded that He be-come their king—for they had long expected a Messiah who, they thought, would establish an earthly kingdom which would rival anything ever before known.

But, determined to carry out the will of His Father, He declined their high offers by explaining that His Kingdom was not of this world. His refusal caused many of His fol-lowers to leave Him, and go back to their former warped beliefs. This was the breaking point—the crisis—in His ministry, for, ere long, He would be traveling alone.

When attention is focused upon the closing days of the ministry of Jesus, we get a mental picture of the day of His triumphant entry into Jerusalem, the city He loved with all His Heart. It was the first time that He publicly declared Himself to be the Messiah, and He received the plaudits of the populace as they acknowledged Him as such. It was to be both a great and terrible time for Him, and He had anticipated it for many seasons.

His entry into Jerusalem was on Palm Sunday, just four days prior to the most unfair, illegal "trials" in the history of civilization. But instead of being a "triumphant occasion," it was to be a dismal day in His earthly experiences.

We see Him mount the small but strong colt of an ass, in keeping with the prophecies, as He begins His trip down the Mount of Olives into Jerusalem's main thoroughfare.

He is greeted by a great multitude who begin spreading

their garments on the ground over which He was to pass. Others cut the branches from trees nearby and strewed the roadway with them to celebrate His coming. Then the multitudes begin to shout:

> Hosanna; Blessed is he that cometh in the name of the Lord: Blessed be the kingdom of our father David, that cometh in the name of the Lord: Hosanna in the highest. [148]

The Pharisees do not appreciate this manifestation of esteem and affection for Christ. They become jealous as they spoke to Christ, *"Master, rebuke thy disciples."*[149]

But Jesus replied:

> I tell you that, if these should hold their peace, the stones would immediately cry out. [150]

Jesus was telling them that this was to be His great day, and that even if He succeeded in making the multitudes become quiet, the stones in the streets would cry out in glorification of Him. So, filled with bitter disappointment, the Pharisees exclaimed:

> Perceive ye how ye prevail nothing? behold, the world is gone after him. [151]

They held a quickly-arranged secret meeting as they laid plans to obtain "false witnesses" to testify against Him. Jesus knew of their conspiracy, for He could read their hearts and minds, as He had so often before done.

---

148) Mark 11:9-10.
149) Luke 19:39.
150) Luke 19:40.
151) John 12:19.

But the crowds began to desert Jesus when they saw Him heading straight for the Temple of God. They had hoped he would go to Herod's palace and fulfill their hopes that He would establish an earthly kingdom.

Observing that His erstwhile followers were fast deserting Him, He wept in loud lamentation as He prophesied the total destruction of Jerusalem.

After spending a short while in the Temple, He left for the village of Bethany because He was hungry and tired. And He wanted to spend one more evening with His beloved friends, Martha, Mary and Lazarus. Therefore, with His twelve disciples, He headed to that little comfortable home to spend the night. He would return to Jerusalem and the Temple the next morning.

Early the next morning we see Him enter the Temple. In a moment, He is filled with rage. Before Him are the hirelings of Annas, selling doves and lambs, and exchanging the Jewish coins for Roman currency—right in the center of the House of God. Taking a whip in His hands, He ran them out into the street, saying:

> It is written, My house shall be called the
> house of prayer; but ye have made it a den
> of thieves. [152]

That was the last straw. Jesus had the audacity to chase the money-changers from the Temple, to the great humiliation of Annas and Caiaphas, who had placed them there for profit.

---

152) Matthew 21:13. See also Mark 11:17; Luke 19:46.

Moreover, only a few days before, Jesus had brought Lazarus back to life in the presence of hundreds of witnesses. All that Annas and his Sadducee friends had taught for hundreds of years—that there was no such thing as the resurrection—had now been repudiated by Jesus.

Annas and the high priest thought something must be done. So they agreed to get Judas Iscariot to betray Jesus so they could murder Him.

Judas had become greatly disillusioned. Like so many other followers of Jesus, he felt that since Jesus had refused to become their earthly king and set up a magnificent palace in Jerusalem, there was no point in remaining loyal.

Moreover, he concluded, in his desperation, that it was time to get what he could, as quickly as possible. Hence he was ready and willing when Annas and Caiaphas made him the proposal to betray his best Friend and Master for thirty pieces of silver. The bargain was sealed and the conspiracy completed.

However, they were not acting as secretly as they thought because Christ knew their plan full well. Matthew, Mark and Luke all tell us that two days before the Feast of the Passover Jesus said to His disciples:

> Ye know that after two days is the feast of the passover, and the Son of man is betrayed to be crucified. [153]

This statement was made just days before His crucifixion. Incidentally, it was the same day that Judas accepted

---

153) Matthew 26:2.

the thirty pieces of silver for assuming the role of a betrayer. Annas and Caiaphas had arranged for Judas to meet them in the palace of the high priest for that very purpose. It was then agreed that Jesus would be apprehended after midnight as He was leaving the Garden of Gethsemane.

Of course, it was plain to the Master that in a matter of a few hours, his earthly ministry would be terminated. Knowing that the shadows of the cross were falling swiftly, He needed to make final preparations for His hour of ordeal and the crucifixion on Calvary.

The unceasing strife and unrest, which had been so prevalent among many of Christ's followers and all those who rejected Him during His three years of teaching, were showing signs of increased intensity. One could feel in the atmosphere around Jerusalem a sense of gloom as little groups were heard to whisper that Jesus would soon be nailed to a cross to die.

But with the Master there was to be no compromise with truth. He was the bravest among the brave—and He knew that His Heavenly Father would sustain Him through the dark moments of anguish when, to others, it might appear that He was friendless and abandoned. Yes, He would silently submit to their insults and physical torture because, in the end, He would be the victor as He took His place on the right hand side of Almighty God.

It can be said that the Master went to Golgotha with a broken heart. All of His efforts to seek and save the lost had been far from successful, and He appreciated this fact to the fullest extent.

It was no surprise to Him when, after the arrest, His disciples forsook Him and fled. He had already told them they would do so. And true to His prophecy, they gathered their garments and slid silently away under the darkness, as they watched the Son of God being led away alone, bound like a common criminal.

Without questioning His Divinity, it would be well to keep in mind His human character as well. For one can then better appreciate the sad picture of His suffering during those last days of His mission—as He determined to carry out the will of the One Who had sent Him. The intense suffering to which He was so brutally subjected was real—He was possessed with a human form made, like us, in the Image of God.

Consider the anguish which must have filled His heart as He wept real tears over the disappointment of His reception in Jerusalem—not the silent weeping which He had done at the cold and silent grave of His beloved friend, Lazarus; but with loud and deep lamentation. [154]

The Master wept because those whom He sought to save turned a deaf ear to His pleadings that they permit Him to be their Saviour and King.

What a heart-rending spectacle! The Son of God weeping, while those He tried to help and save were busy plotting His destruction —for no reason except their failure to understand the true purpose of His ministry.

His great love for humanity, including the vilest sin-

---

154) Matthew 23:37.

ners, was akin to the passionate intensity of a devoted mother who nurtures and protects her helpless babes.

Despite Christ's loving attitude, their hearts were as hard as stone, their wills stubborn, and their ears dulled by the cowardly chants of those who preferred to slay rather than praise the Son of God.

It was the Apostle John, whose writings always thrill the hungered soul, who said of the Master, *"He came unto his own, and his own received him not."*[155]

Then came the evening appointed for Jesus to observe the Feast of the Passover with His disciples, when every Jew would be also celebrating as a memorial to God's deliverance of the children of Israel from bondage. Therefore, the Master repaired to the "upper chamber" for the last supper—His final meal on earth before His death.

This was also a momentous re-enactment of that last night in Egypt before the great Exodus, and was intended as a symbol of lasting gratitude for that deliverance.

But there was one present at that final meal whose heart no longer knew the meaning of gratitude—for Judas Iscariot, his pocket bulging with the evil money for betrayal, was told by Christ that it was he who would perform the act of treachery. Judas had the gall to pretend innocence, and to sit there and let Christ wash his putrid feet, as though he were still a loyal follower of the Master.

Yes, this Memorial supper was to be to His followers everything that the Passover had been to Israel. It was

---

155) John 1:11.

to forever commemorate His death, without which there would have been no redemption. So He advised His disciples, *"This do in remembrance of me."*[156]

With the heavy burdens of a lost world pressing heavily upon Him, we see Jesus Christ, with eleven of His disciples, proceeding to the Garden for prayer to His Father. Judas was not there because he had slipped out to notify the murderers where Jesus might be found.

As He reached the place in the Garden where He wanted the disciples to remain, He instructed them to, *"Sit ye here, while I go and pray yonder."*[157]

Then, like He had done many times before, He called for Peter, James and John to go deeper into the Garden with Him, saying:

> My soul is exceeding sorrowful, even unto death: tarry ye here, and watch with me. [158]

For some reason, none of the disciples could remain awake to watch while Christ was so deep in prayer. Three times Jesus came to them, and each time He found them sound asleep. Finally, He awoke them and said:

> Sleep on now, and take your rest: it is enough, the hour is come; behold the Son of man is betrayed into the hands of sinners. Rise up, let us go; lo, he that betrayeth me is at hand. [159]

---

156) Luke 22:19. See also 1 Corinthians 11:24.
157) Matthew 26:36. See also Mark 14:32.
158) Matthew 26:38.
159) Mark 14:41-42.

Then came forth the despicable Judas, who planted the traitor's kiss upon Jesus' cheek as a signal for them to seize Him. The Master was perfectly calm as He ridiculed His erstwhile disciple with this statement:

> Judas, betrayest thou the Son of man with a kiss? [160]

Already Judas was filled with a deep consciousness of his terrible mistake because in a matter of hours he had committed suicide by causing his head to dangle from the end of a sturdy rope upon the public highway.

We remember, of course, those later events which led to the crucifixion. From that moment forward, the shadows of the cross were falling with increased swiftness. And through it all, Jesus Christ remained silent, meek, calm and courageous.

---

160) Luke 22:48.

CHAPTER 21

ARGUMENT ON LAW AND THE FACTS

When Jesus was tried, the system of selection of a group of men to decide the issues of fact in criminal or civil cases was unknown. Therefore, Jesus was tried before the judges of the Sanhedrin without benefit of counsel or a jury. This was also true in respect to the trial before the Roman Governor, Pontius Pilate.

Moreover, any person found guilty of an offense before the Sanhedrin could, if dissatisfied with the verdict, obtain an immediate appeal to the Emperor. The one exception, however, applied to the Jews. They did not enjoy that privilege, for it was reserved only for the Roman citizen.

We recall that Saul of Tarsus, after his conviction before the Jewish courts, was granted an appeal to Caesar, because he enjoyed the rights of a Roman citizen. [161] To say the least, that was a harsh and unfair rule of the law-makers of Jewish society, which they were required to create in response to the demands of their Roman conquerors. It was

---

161) See Acts 25:11-12. See also Acts 22:25-29.

discrimination against a particular race who happened to be subjected to penalties such as that because they were the conquered people.

The above explanation seems in order so the reader will not feel that two other errors might have been committed during the trial of the Master—not having counsel to represent Him, and not having a jury to hear the evidence and decide the factual issues.

We come now to a summation relative to the laws and the testimony sought by the prosecution against Christ.

It is our purpose in this closing chapter to discuss those eighteen separate errors which were deliberately committed by those who pretended to give Jesus His "trials."

We have already cited the applicable Hebrew laws which were in force during the trials; and the manner in which He was treated has been set forth, as reflected in the true accounts of Matthew, Mark, Luke and John.

1. Illegal Apprehension

The first unlawful act was the apprehension of Jesus by the multitude led by Judas Iscariot, as they came forth with their lanterns, torches and staves, and met Christ as He concluded His prayers to His Heavenly Father, and was leaving the Garden of Gethsemane.

As Judas and his mob of Roman soldiers and servants from the palace of the high priest came within speaking distance with Christ, He inquired of whom they were seeking; and when they said "Jesus of Nazareth," It was then that Judas came closer and planted the betrayer's kiss upon the cheek of Jesus Christ—not as the customary token of esteem and friendship, but as a signal for the soldiers and servants of Caiaphas to seize Him.

Judas, the man in charge of the "multitude," stood there while they bound Him with strong cords of rope. Never once did he state to the Master, nor show to Him, any lawful commission or authority from the high priest, or any other legal power, which would have made the arrest legal.

The binding of Christ was done by the great multitude who had swords and staves and torches. Little did it matter to that arch traitor that, in coming to the gate of the Garden to consummate his evil bargain, he was guiding the mob to the hallowed sanctuary of the Son of God.

Nor was he the least concerned over his deliberate profaning of the Passover, which, to the Jews, was the most sacred season of the entire year.

After having effected the illegal arrest, they did not even tell Jesus for what He was being apprehended. Of course, He, in His Infinite Wisdom, did know that it was in consequence of the conspiracy to take Him by trickery and to try Him in the absence of His friends.

Judas no doubt felt that he was bigger than the laws of Jewry; and that since he had now aligned himself with the high priest and Annas, no harm could come to him.

Of course, we know that Jesus voluntarily submitted to those He called "sinners." And He reminded them at the time of His arrest that He could easily resist their pitiful efforts should He so desire:

> Thinkest thou that I cannot now pray to my
> Father, and he shall presently give me more
> than twelve legions of angels? [162]

He did not ask for the legions of angels because He was more than willing to do the will of His Father. He was ready to make the supreme sacrifice and thereby become the means of having the holy Scriptures fulfilled. Nothing else was of any concern to Him.

Some may inquire: "When He submitted voluntarily to the arrest, did not that make it legal?" The answer is far from difficult, because once an act is unlawfully done, no voluntary movement by another could possibly breathe legality into it.

2. No Jurisdiction

The second unlawful act was committed when they bound Jesus and hailed Him before Annas, the political boss of Judea. Annas, being without any judicial or ecclesiastical position within the Jewish society, had absolutely no jurisdiction over Christ.

Furthermore, the law prohibited the taking of any prisoner before any individual—even a judge—for a private examination. But since Annas was one of the chief parties of the conspiracy between Judas and Caiaphas, he wished to have personal knowledge of the arrest so he might get Caiaphas to call that secret, select crowd of judges of the Sanhedrin that they might "try" Jesus under cover of darkness.

---

162) Matthew 26:53.

As soon as they had brought the Master to the house of Annas, he got the word to the high priest to begin the unlawful assembling of the Sanhedrin.

Annas' chief motive in desiring to be rid of Jesus was based on the fact that Jesus had proved the fact of the resurrection, in spite of the contrary teachings and belief of Annas who, for some sixty years preached a creed that there was no such thing as life beyond the grave, nor future rewards and punishments.

Also, we recall that it was the hirelings of Annas who sold the lambs and doves, and were the money-changers within the Temple of God, and that Jesus had the courage and fortitude to run them into the streets with a whip as He rightly accused them of desecrating the House of Prayer by making it a virtual den of thieves.

Naturally, that made Annas furious because no longer would he receive the large profits from those unholy operations, in complete defiance of the laws of God, as well as the laws of man. He felt that he had been embarrassed and humiliated by the teachings and proofs being offered by Jesus that the dogma and creed of Annas and his followers were without substance or truth.

The influence wielded by Annas upon the high priest, as well as all the others who perpetrated those horrible crimes in dealing with Jesus, was largely responsible for the open and repeated unlawful acts. He was the brains behind the sordid plan and conspiracy to abruptly terminate the ministry of Christ by having Him crucified.

He may not have held the hammer which drove the

nails into the precious hands and feet of Jesus, but he was there to see that it was done, as he bossed the proceedings from the first to the last stages of that horrible drama.

We shall now discuss briefly the fact that the members of the Sanhedrin were disqualified to participate in the trial of Jesus because of their known enmity toward Him.

The full membership of the Sanhedrin was seventy-one. But on the night Jesus was tried, they had purposely selected only a bare quorum of twenty-three members, practically all of whom were related to Annas, including his five sons and son-in-law.

We remember that the Hebrew laws forbade any member of the Sanhedrin from sitting thereon during the trial of a case where there existed enmity between any judge and the accused before the bar. Here is the exact language of the Jewish Code:

> Nor under any circumstances, was a man
> known to be at enmity with the accused per-
> son permitted to occupy a position among
> the judges.

That was a good law. It protected some unfortunate person from being tried before judges who were his enemy. What measure of justice could one expect to receive in such circumstances? Such a judge would, whether conscious of it or not, lean toward the prosecution at all events.

He may not necessarily be inherently corrupt, but he would be greatly influenced by prejudice.

3. Unqualified Judges

How about those twenty-three select members of that Sanhedrin? Were they qualified under the above quoted Hebrew Law to sit as judges when Christ was on trial? They were the very crowd who boasted of seeking "false witnesses" that they might condemn Jesus to die, even before the trial had started. They arranged the details of the conspiracy with Judas to the end that Christ might be apprehended and brought before them almost immediately thereafter, while the Lord's friends and followers were asleep.

Are we to be surprised to read that there was not a dissenting voice raised when the high priest, Caiaphas, condemned Jesus for "blasphemy" and asked his fellow-judges how they voted? No wonder they *all condemned him to be guilty of death.* "[163]

They were no more than mere tools and cowardly puppets of Annas and Caiaphas. No longer were they permitted to think for themselves, to weigh the evidence, and vote their honest convictions on the guilt or innocence of Christ. How sad to see one becoming a "rubber stamp" while wearing the garb of a member of the judiciary.

Worse still, they were members of the Supreme Court of Jewry, the highest court in the land. And they disgraced the high office by their corruption and cowardice.

While it is true that Jesus submitted, as a volunteer, to their wrongful and spiteful acts, because He well knew it all was in keeping with the prophecies concerning the Son

---

163) Mark 14:64.

of God; yet, except for that fact, there still remains a blight on the erstwhile good name of the Sanhedrin. They were acting as evil-minded men—with murder in their hearts, and hatred in their souls.

4. Court Assembled Unlawfully

There is now assigned, as the fourth error, the proposition that the Jewish court was assembled unlawfully.

The laws prohibited the Sanhedrin from meeting on the day before a Sabbath, at night, or during the celebration of the Feast of the Passover. It was between two and two—thirty o'clock after midnight when they assembled.

He was tried, condemned and crucified all in one day, and certainly all have admitted that the Feast of the Passover was then in progress. Thousands of pilgrims had filled Jerusalem, prepared to celebrate that Feast.

What then do we have, relative to the unlawful assembling of the highest Jewish court? Every member—with full knowledge of the laws—broke three separate provisions of their own Code.

Let those who, though in a very inconsequential minority, seek to justify the attitude and conduct of the members of the Sanhedrin dare challenge those three violations of the Hebrew laws. None have been able to do so after two thousand years.

One might, with borrowed compassion, seek to forgive them for those three violations of their own laws; but, when we continue the review of the other and more serious transgressions, done with the same evil spirit and murderous intentions, we note every evidence of willfulness and premeditation born of a corrupt design.

The creation of humane and justice-giving laws, for the high purpose of protecting the innocent, as well as insuring fairness to all accused, is one thing; but, the manner in which those beneficial statutes are applied and enforced, or ignominiously trampled upon, is quite another. Those laws of the Jews were meant to be enforced and respected. And, when Jesus was to be tried, there should have been no exception.

5. No Charges Against Jesus

When Jesus was brought before the Sanhedrin for "trial," no one had proffered a single charge against Him. The charge of "blasphemy" made by the high priest some thirty minutes after the trial had started was most irregular as well as illegal.

If, at the beginning of the proceedings, no accusations were then pending against Christ, then why was the Sanhedrin assembled at that hour in the night? And with equal logic and reasoning, how could He or anyone be called on to stand "trial" for His life when no man had accused the Prisoner?

It is noteworthy that, at that dark hour of the early morning, there was no other business before the Sanhedrin. It was called into that nocturnal, secret session for only one purpose—to "try" Jesus Christ. Then we ask, *"Try Him for what?"* The only answer can be found in the realization that they met at that hour to execute their dastardly scheme to rob Him of every legal right. He was to be condemned to die for no reason except that those evil-minded men had already agreed among themselves two days earlier that they would murder Him.

Was not that a despicable sight to behold—twenty-three weather-beaten countenances giving off their cowardly reflections against the delicate glow of God's moonlight—as they await the arrival of the weary Christ, that they might subject Him to what they called a "trial."

What a mockery! What a farce! What a searing travesty upon the glorious name of justice, decency and fairness. God forbid! We could wish that the sordid record of their cheap scheming and cowardly crimes might never have been implanted among the beautiful and inspiring passages of the Word of God.

But we know that the narrations are true. The men who witnessed this tragedy were influenced by the all-powerful voice of our Heavenly Father to write on those pages what they had seen so that the generations yet unborn might understand the full measure of the price the Son of God voluntarily paid to redeem mankind.

6. Two Witnesses

When the highest court of the Jews deliberately failed to produce the required two witnesses to testify against Jesus, they committed the sixth error of the tragic trial.

We reverently turn back the musty pages of Mosaic law, relative to the required number of witnesses for the prosecution, and find this language:

At the mouth of two witnesses, or three witnesses, shall he that is worthy of death be put to death; but at the mouth of one witness he shall not be put to death. [164]

Where were the *"two witnesses"* to establish that Jesus was guilty of "blasphemy"? They did not have even one witness. And even if they had *one* witness, the Hebrew law prohibited the taking of human life thereby. But even without the one, they took the law into their murderous hands and applied it to suit the insatiable desires of their corrupt hearts and minds.

Finding themselves unable to garner any witnesses against the Master, the high priest, Caiaphas, willfully disobeyed the ninth commandment of God, *"Thou shalt not bear false witness against thy neighbor."*[165]

He, we recall, was the only so-called witness against Jesus, who absurdly accused Christ of "blasphemy" without a word of proof to support his conclusion. It is almost inconceivable that Caiaphas could sufficiently insulate himself against the flaming jaws of Hell and eternal damnation.

No character participating in those "trials" of Jesus is worthy of greater condemnation than the debased fiend, Caiaphas. Jesus Himself measured the extent of the sin of Caiaphas when, before Pilate, He referred to the high priest as the one who had delivered Jesus to the Roman Governor, and said, *"...he that delivered me unto thee hath the*

---

164) Deuteronomy 17:6. See also Deuteronomy 19:15.
165) Exodus 20:16. See also Deuteronomy 5:20.

greater sin. "[166] The mention of his name is an abomination. So we pass on.

7. Absence of Jurisdiction

All courts are limited in the scope of their jurisdiction. The seventh error of law is found in the absence of jurisdiction of the Sanhedrin. Until a prisoner has first been lawfully arrested, a court cannot legally acquire any jurisdiction over his person.

As we revert to the unlawful arrest of Jesus, it follows that they had no right to try Him until jurisdiction had been acquired in consequence of a legal apprehension. Annas and the high priest were well aware of the conditions of that arrest. They had planned for Him to be taken without a warrant of arrest, when no charges had been filed before them.

Having personal knowledge of an unlawful arrest, they wrongfully took jurisdiction of Jesus Christ. But with them it made no difference. They were not there to insure any safeguards for Jesus, even though the Hebrew laws so provided.

Any judgment, verdict or sentence imposed by a court devoid of jurisdiction of either the subject matter of the inquiry, or the person of the accused, would, in law, be a nullity, and void. Such was the true status of the sentence and condemnation of Jesus by the Sanhedrin.

---

166) John 19:11.

8. Lack of Witnesses

The eighth error is that those who tried Christ did not produce any witnesses to establish the fact that Jesus did not speak the truth when He admitted to being the Son of God.

The burden of proof was upon them to establish by the testimony and evidence, beyond a reasonable doubt, and to a moral certainty, that He was not as He had represented.

In other words, when Jesus stated that He was the Son of God, and they took the opposite view, it was proper for the members of the Jewish court to prove otherwise.

If Christ spoke the truth, He certainly could not be condemned by anyone. If, on the other hand, He did not, they should have introduced testimony on that issue. He was accused of "blasphemy," and condemned for it—yet they did nothing to establish His guilt.

This is just another illustration of the high-handed, evil- spirited tactics employed by the Sanhedrin membership by judges learned in the Hebrew laws—by judges sworn to uphold those laws. Rules of evidence, when Jesus was before them, were of no consequence. To convict Him they had to deliberately ignore all existing laws, and they did so without remorse of conscience.

9. Changing The Charges

Changing the charges against the accused without notice to him after the "trial" had begun was unheard of in judicial proceedings under the Hebrew laws. Thus they committed the ninth error.

Looking back to the trials, we recall that the first charge against Jesus was made by the false witnesses who said that Christ had threatened to destroy the Temple of God and raise it up again in three days.

When those charges were found to be untrue and absurd, they were no longer considered by the Sanhedrin. It was then that the high priest changed the charge to "blasphemy."

Then, before the Roman Governor, they changed it again to "sedition," under the false premise that Jesus had been stirring up the nation and teaching that one should no longer pay tribute to the Emperor.

Then, while before Pilate, they accused Him of claiming to be the King. With no notice to the Master, they made four separate charges against Him, while the "trials" were in progress.

One would naturally conclude that with such outlandish tactics, they were on a "fishing expedition," trying to make any kind of accusation, hoping ultimately to convince the Governor of Judea that their Prisoner had committed some offense for which He should suffer the penalty of death.

Could one imagine a more absurdly illegal proceeding than this? Suppose a man was brought into court, charged with murder. When the proof failed, they then charged him with grand larceny. When the proof was found not sufficient, they then changed it to rape. When they could not substantiate that charge, they then accused him of burglary.

Anyone would say that such a thing would be manifestly unfair and unlawful. But that is exactly what they did during the trials of Jesus, except that the numerous charges were of a different nature. The principle, however, was the same.

The series of charge-switching was in direct conflict with the laws of the Jewish nation, for under the Hebrew Code of procedure such action was considered intolerable and wholly without legal support.

10. No Witnesses Allowed for Jesus

The tenth reason assigned as error springs from the fact that the proceedings were of a one-sided nature, since Christ was not given opportunity to corroborate His contention that He was the Son of God.

We know that He could have had thousands present to testify to that truth. To deny Him that well-settled right was another illustration of how determined they were to destroy Him, with no regard for legal procedure or justice.

No one knew better than the members of the Sanhedrin that Christ could have, on very short notice, summoned a host of His followers and beneficiaries of His miracles to testify that no one but the Son of God could have done such things.

Being personally acquainted with a vast majority of those wonderful miracles of Christ, they were sorely afraid to meet the issue of whether He was a Divine Being. The law gave Jesus that right, but they took it away from Him, without reason. To have afforded Him such an opportunity would have foiled their plans to kill Him.

11. No Corroborating Witness

The eleventh error resulted from their condemnation of Jesus solely upon His Own confession that He was the Son of God. When they failed to produce a single witness against Jesus, He was entitled to an acquittal because of the requirement of at least two witnesses. When the only evidence before the Sanhedrin was the uncorroborated admission of Christ, they violated their own laws by condemning Him to die.

> A voluntary confession on his part is not admitted in evidence, and therefore, not competent to convict, unless a legal number of witnesses minutely corroborate his self accusation.

As the presiding judge of the Sanhedrin, Caiaphas knew full well that there was no corroboration, yet he shouted the judgment of condemnation. And his puppets, the other "judges" of that Jewish court, were evidently afraid to vote in opposition.

12. Trial Concluded in One Day

For the twelfth error, we cite the following law:

> A criminal case, where a death sentence is to be pronounced, cannot be concluded before the following day.

The trial of Jesus was concluded in a few hours, although under the law it was required to be carried forward into the second day.

13. Jesus Denied a Defense

After having been accused and then immediately condemned for "blasphemy," Jesus should have been permitted to offer His defense to the accusation. Denying Him that privilege is the thirteenth error. It was high-handed, to say the least, for the Sanhedrin to falsely condemn Christ, then deny Him the right to submit His defense. Since they were determined to keep the proceedings as one-sided as possible by violating every known law, they did so.

When the Sanhedrin announced their unanimous agreement to the verdict of guilty of "blasphemy," they did so in the face of the solemn Jewish laws to the contrary. The Hebrew Code provided that a unanimous verdict against the accused would result in his acquittal.

14. Unanimous Equals Acquittal

Legally, Jesus was entitled to His immediate release when all twenty-three members of the Sanhedrin voted in approval of the condemnation announced by the high priest. This was the fourteenth error.

15. Jesus Taken Before Herod

The fifteenth error was when the Sanhedrin, by the directions of Pilate, took Jesus before King Herod. That man had no jurisdiction, for at that stage of the proceedings no lawful charge had been preferred against the Master. Therefore, there was nothing for Herod to consider or decide. That is the main reason why Herod, without condemning Jesus, sent Him back to Pilate.

They had no reason to take Jesus there, except the hope

that Herod, who had previously threatened to kill Jesus, might direct His execution, since it was then doubtful that Pilate would do so.

16. Crucifixion Without Authority

Although the Jewish court had no authority to execute anyone, they condemned Jesus to die, and crucified Him, although the Roman Governor had not approved such a sentence. That was the sixteenth error.

If they had obtained the legal authority to take the life of Jesus, which Caiaphas, before Pilate, admitted they did not have, then there would have been no point in delaying His execution by taking Him before the Roman Governor.

17. Jesus Taken Before Roman Governor

By several of the previously mentioned errors, the Sanhedrin wrongfully condemned Jesus without lawful authority. Thus, they committed the seventeenth error by taking Him before the Roman Governor to approve what their own laws declared to be illegal and void.

Knowing that their acts were illegal, they endeavored to shift the responsibility to the shoulders of the Roman Governor. They wanted him to give the official orders for the execution of Jesus, since they could not do so themselves.

18. Not Guilty — Execute Him!

Except for the trial of Jesus, it was unheard of for a judge to find a man not guilty and then deliver him over for execution. But that is what Pilate did with the Master.

Four separate times he publicly declared that he had found Jesus guilty of nothing. But in spite of that, he illegally delivered Jesus to the mob to be crucified. The members of the Sanhedrin spitefully ignored every known Jewish law in their efforts to take His life. Then, as a climax, they crucified Christ. To say the least, their acts were cold-blooded murder.

Examination of The Facts

After His illegal arrest, Jesus was first taken before Annas, who was the "power behind the throne," as far as the high priest was concerned. The political boss of Judea asked Jesus about His teachings, and His disciples. But the Master remained silent, which was His legal right. But when Annas persisted about His doctrines, Jesus replied:

> I spake openly to the world; I ever taught in the synagogue, and in the temple, whither the Jews always resort; and in secret have I said nothing. Why askest thou me? ask them which heard me, what I have said unto them: behold, they know what I said. [167]

Jesus was merely stating that He had never spoken in secret, and that all of His doctrines had been expounded in the public places of worship. And if a check on His creed was desired, just ask those who had heard Him.

That was a logical statement, but it irritated Annas. He saw that he was getting nowhere with his unlawful examination.

---

167) John 18:20-21.

Then came the first act of physical violence. One of the servants of Annas, realizing that Jesus had put Annas in a ridiculous light, struck Christ an insulting blow in the face. Then the servant inquired of the Master, *"Answerest thou the high priest so?"*[168]

That servile laborer of the house of Annas was under the false impression that his boss was *still* the "high priest." No doubt Annas had made them think so because of his dictatorial handling of that office for so long, as well as his domination over the *real* high priest, his son-in-law, Caiaphas.

Such an outburst of temper should have called for immediate dismissal of the servant, but Annas, according to records, made no complaint about this outrage. Then, after silently submitting to the coward's blow, Jesus said:

> If I have spoken evil, bear witness of the evil: but if well, why smitest thou me?[169]

168) John 18:22.
169) John 18:23.

Christ was well versed in Hebrew laws. He was telling them if He had spoken improperly, then be a witness to it, but otherwise why do you strike Me?

Neither Annas nor anyone else could reply to that inquiry of Jesus. So to save further embarrassment, Annas directed that Christ be taken before the Sanhedrin, which by now was in the process of unlawfully assembling, with a bare quorum of twenty-three carefully selected members, in keeping with their conspiracy. They would be ready, for their minds had been made up for some time.

The first blow upon the Body of Jesus by the servant of Annas was only the start of a series of brutalities which were to be inflicted. As the Master had said, He was now in the hands of sinful men.

To make sure that there would be no slip-up or delay in the proceedings, Annas led the unholy procession about two blocks from his home through the dark streets of Jerusalem to the Sanhedrin.

We recall how they attempted to use the testimony of their own false witnesses, and that their statements were discredited. Then, in desperation, the high priest, visibly affected by the calmness of the Master, left his seat and ran toward Jesus, his voice filled with hatred, and said:

> I adjure thee by the living God, that thou
> tell us whether thou be the Christ, the Son
> of God. [170]

Until now Jesus had maintained silence. But now He

---

170) Matthew 26:63.

certainly must speak out. He must reaffirm what He had so often told the people—that He was the Son of God. He knew that to claim equality with God, if untrue, would be blasphemy. Therefore, He clearly admitted being the Son of God by answering the high priest, saying:

> I am: and ye shall see the Son of man sitting
> on the right hand of power, and coming in
> the clouds of heaven. [171]

Without a moments hesitation, Caiaphas ripped his own robe almost into shreds. Then in a loud voice he said:

> He hath spoken blasphemy; what further
> need have we of witnesses? behold, now ye
> have heard his blasphemy. What think ye? [172]

Being of one accord, they all condemned Him to be worthy of death. But before leaving for the Praetorium of Pilate to get their death sentence approved, they arose against Him in a great rebellion, and hurled insult after insult, and blow after blow with intensified coarseness and ferocity. It was, beyond doubt, the most disgraceful spectacle ever witnessed in any court in all the world. Take a glance at what transpired in the very center of the Supreme Court of Jewry, the highest court within the Jewish society.

> Then did they spit in his face, and buffeted
> him; and others smote him with the palms
> of their hands, [173]

---

171) Mark 14:62.
172) Matthew 26:65-66.
173) Matthew 26:67.

And they blindfolded Him[174] and said:

> Prophesy unto us, thou Christ, Who is he
> that smote thee?[175]

But there stood Jesus, silently submissive. Not defense-less, but not defending. Not helpless, in the sense that He was forced to take their harsh punishment, but not con-tending. His voluntary submission was majestic evidence of a Son's devotion to His Father's will.

Why did they conduct themselves like wild, depraved culprits? Because even before they had met on that morn-ing, they had a single purpose; not to give Christ a legal trial, but to conduct a hurried, judicial murder. The Master was already convicted before the lights of the courtroom were lit. They were there only to determine how the unlaw-ful sentence of death might be put into effect.

If they had the power to kill Christ they would never have taken Him before Pilate. They knew that when they were before the Governor, he would ridicule them for hav-ing sentenced Jesus to death without any proof of any wrongdoing.

Therefore, they changed the accusation from "blas-phemy" to "sedition," by claiming that Christ advocated disloyalty to the Roman Emperor by teaching that it was unlawful to continue paying tribute to Caesar, and by claiming to be a king.

Why did they stop at the gate of the Praetorium of

---

174) See Luke 22:64.
175) Matthew 26:68.

Pilate? Because under their religious beliefs it would have been an act of defilement to enter that building during the Feast of the Passover. It was alright to commit murder, but not to become defiled by entering the Praetorium. Such was the reasoning of those depraved mortals.

That which took place before the Roman Governor is still fresh in our minds. On four separate occasions, Pilate stated that Jesus should be released because he had found Him guilty of nothing. It was only through fear of losing his political job that he finally acted the role of a coward by delivering Jesus to the raving mob to be crucified. Pilate sought to "wash his hands" as a symbol of non-guilt, but the relentless clock of time has not yet removed the stain of Innocent Blood.

As we follow Christ's hallowed path from the Praetorium of Pilate to the crest of Calvary's hill, we note that the same mob of evil-minded men persisted in the brutalities as they gave vent to their hatred of the Son of God.

As may be expected, Annas and Caiaphas were leading the procession, giving directions, inciting the bystanders to increase the size of the mob, and finally, showing the Roman soldiers how to produce the greatest pain as they mutilated and later crucified the precious Body of the Son of God.

We next witness Christ leaving the court of Pilate, having been delivered over for the march to Golgotha's hill. Still in the presence of the Roman Governor, Jesus is roughly handled by the low-bred, coarse soldiers and servants of the high priest.

After whipping Him until the blood gushed from His back, chest and arms, they placed upon Him an old, dilapidated, purple robe —the symbol of ridicule and scorn. Then they forced into His hands a crude reed to represent a king's scepter —all in further ridicule of His claim to be a king.

But that is not all. They imbedded a crown of sharp thorns so deeply into His brow that the blood filled His precious eyes to where He could not see. Still not sure that the thorns were deep enough to produce great pain, they struck Him with sticks over the thorny crown.

Then, with Christ hardly able to stand up, and unable to see, they took turns spitting in His face and striking Him on the head.

Those acts of inhuman brutality took place at the front entrance to the palace of the Roman Governor, Pilate, who had given his approval by his silence. It was Pilate upon whose shoulders rested the sole responsibility for the general welfare and best interest of the citizens within Judea —and he smilingly approved of *that.*

This indictment will forever be registered against Pontius Pilate:

1. He ignored his personal knowledge of the innocence of Jesus, and delivered Him over to the mob to be crucified.

2. He cast to the winds the solemn warnings of his wife to have nothing to do with an Innocent Man.

3. Having full authority to release Jesus, he became one of the actors in the awful drama of cold-blooded murder.

4. He played the part of a lowbrow coward, when test

of character, honor, decency and justice was on trial, by trying to dismiss his guilt through the pitiful symbol of "washing his hands" of the Innocent Blood.

5. He cowardly surrendered the authority and dignity of the high office of Governor of Judea by becoming afraid of the cruel-hearted demands of a murderous gang.

6. Rather than risk being removed from office by a band of angered Jews, he gave up custody of an Innocent person, with full knowledge that He was to be crucified.

Let us look at the scene leading to Calvary on that morning:

It was now about ten o'clock, and Jesus had been deprived of food and sleep. They ignored His fatigue and pain and made Him carry a heavy, rugged cross up the winding slopes to Calvary's hill. The weight of that cross was far more than the normal capacity of the average man, and created a terrible strain upon His already bruised and bleeding shoulders.

The scourging before Pilate had left fresh cuts in the flesh, from which blood was plainly seen to flow. No wonder He stumbled under that great burden, and was blinded from the blood of the crown of thorns, which pressed deeply into His precious brow.

It was the Feast of the Passover, the greatest Feast known to Jewry. They were in Jerusalem by the uncounted thousands. The shops were closed, the streets crowded with men and women, wandering aimlessly in search of diversion. Suddenly their attention was attracted by an unusual procession, the order of which was probably as follows:

In the forefront could be seen a small man, carrying a large banner, with this inscription:

"Jesus of Nazareth the King of the Jews."

Following closely behind, is Jesus. His face pallid and wincing with evidence of great pain and anguish as He labors with all of His might to carry the heavy cross. A few paces behind the Master, we recognize a group of Pharisees and Sadducees who are talking and jesting with Annas, along with Caiaphas. Both widely smile as they take turns waving in acknowledgment to the greetings of their followers who line the streets.

Then comes the band of Roman soldiers and the servants of the high priest—the cruel executioners—with their spears and swords drawn high, as if to again pierce the precious body of the Master, should he, for a fleeting moment, delay the procession in the fulfillment of its unholy assignment.

Just a few feet back we see a multitude of curiosity seekers who had by now multiplied into thousands, for they had also been attracted by this strange parade of death. They knew that there was to be another crucifixion, but little did they dream that it would go down in human history as the most cruel of all.

There, on the right side of Jesus, but considerably to the rear, we see the one remaining disciple, John, as he holds the arm of the mother of Christ, seeking, without success, to console and comfort her in that great hour of grief.

Immediately to her right, and slightly to the rear, is a mere handful of His friends, for all of the other disciples "forsook him and fled."

All along the route, ignorant bigots and drunkards shouted: "Away with him, crucify him, crucify him." How strange that just a few days before, those same voices were on those same streets shouting:

> Blessed is he that cometh in the name of the
> Lord; Hosanna in the highest. [176]

Why the sudden change from praise and adulation to condemnation and vilification? What had He done? Where is the man who had accused Him, and thus made Him guilty of such a cruel death? The answer is summed up in four words: Prejudice, Hatred, Jealousy and Ignorance.

As they wind the weary route up Calvary, Jesus begins to swoon and fall because of the great load, the steep hills, His weakened condition, and the great loss of blood. Rather than delay the forward march to the execution grounds,

---

176) Matthew 21:9.

they had a Cyrenian help Jesus carry the cross. He did not ask for that help because He was able to bear the pain without uttering a single word.

After traveling a short distance, to make sure His burdens were not made any lighter, they ordered Simon to again place the heavy cross upon the bleeding and painfully-sore shoulder of the Son of God.

What a cruel sight to behold upon the principal streets of Jerusalem—the city which was close to the heart of Jesus—the city the Master had recently wept over as He foretold its later destruction. Those tears had hardly dried upon His precious cheeks when plans to destroy Him were being made.

But now others in Jerusalem were weeping. When a group of women beheld the pitiful sight of the Son of God staggering under His burden, with His blood-stained garments sticking to His body, and His eyes filled with blood, they shed their tears without restraint. Christ saw them as they wept, but in that solemn hour, with its pain and anguish, He felt there was no need for tears of sympathy from anyone. As He recalled that prophesy about Jerusalem becoming destroyed, He said to them:

> Daughters of Jerusalem, weep not for me, but weep for yourselves, and for your children. [177]

Yes, there are times when even well-meant sympathy is out of place. On this particular occasion, Jesus did not

---

177) Luke 23:28.

want to be looked upon as an object of pity. For with Him, it was in every sense, the fulfillment of the great object of the world's faith.

He also knew that this type of treatment was to be exacted of Him at that very hour. He had the sustaining grace and power of Almighty God, and nothing else was of any consequence. He would see it through, regardless of the cost or pain.

We come now to Golgotha, called the place of the skull. The two thieves are being placed on their crosses, with their hands and feet *tied* thereon. But with the Master, the strong Roman soldiers begin the bloody assignment of *nailing* the feet and hands of Jesus to His cross.

Why the difference? Why show self-confessed thieves more humane consideration than Jesus? They had confessed their guilt, but no one had proved Jesus guilty of a single wrong. No one could possibly prove Him to be other than the sinless, guiltless Son of God. Despite all this, the crucifixion Jesus suffered was known to be the cruelest death within the knowledge of mankind, producing the most extreme pain —beyond description.

They lifted the bleeding Jesus into an upright position, slightly higher than, and in the middle of, the two thieves. As soon as the cross was secured in the ground, Pilate placed above the head of the dying Christ a title he had written:

> JESUS OF NAZARETH THE KING OF
> THE JEWS. [178]

---

178) John 19:19.

Pilate had the explanatory statement printed in Hebrew, Latin and Greek, so all nationalities among the motley crowd could read it, and join in their mockery.

Jesus had not been suspended upon the cross but a few minutes when the Roman soldiers cast lots for His robe, just as the Scriptures had said would happen.

The dying Christ, filled with indescribable pain, looked down from the cross and, remembering the powerful quality of Divine mercy, He uttered a prayer to His Heavenly Father, asking pardon for His murderers:

Father, forgive them; for they know not what they do.

Standing close by was His mother, her eyes filled with tears as she clasped her hands together, as if in prayer, her eyes trained on her bleeding, suffering precious Son. One could see the attitude of abject helplessness written upon her beautiful face, as she occasionally wiped the welling tears from her swollen eyes.

Next to her was John, the faithful disciple whom Jesus loved. He was still trying to console the broken-hearted mother of Christ.

Next to him we see Nicodemus, Joseph of Arimathaea, Mary Magdalene, Salome, the mother of James and John, Mary, the wife of Cleophas, Joanna, the wife of Chuza… and maybe a handful more.

The Mockery Continues

Wishing to bring as much pain as possible to the Master, the cruel tormenters shout outbursts of vile mockery. They loudly ridicule Him and laugh at His claim of being the Son of God, daring Him to come down from the cross and prove His claims. The same gang who so miserably disgraced the Sanhedrin were the loudest in their ridicule, saying:

He saved others; himself he cannot save. [179]

Through all the torture and insults hurled at the dying Christ, He showed His limitless bravery and submission. When we consider His human qualities, we know that His experience of pain was violent beyond imagination.

It is common knowledge that when one has lost a large quantity of blood, there is an insatiable desire for water. The terrible feeling of absolute dryness of the tongue, and the sense of parching of the throat aggravates the longing for some kind of liquid. When Jesus was outstretched upon that cross and virtually dying, He cried out, *"I thirst."*[180]

Oh, what anguish that thirst must have produced, making it the more difficult for Him to even cry for water. And what brutality it was to deny Him just a few drops of

179) Matthew 27:42 & Mark 15:31. See also Luke 23:35.
180) John 19:28.

cool water. But no! They were not there to pacify the Sufferer, nor to cool the raging fever of His swollen tongue and throat. Their mission was to add pain and anguish. It is incredible what black hearts will sometimes make men stoop to do.

Let the reader pause for a moment and reflect upon that barbaric scene at Calvary:

We see Jesus Christ, the Son of God, His arms stretched outward, with His hands and feet brutally nailed to the cross. A large quantity of blood is pouring forth from His wounds, so much so that the clothes covering His lower extremities are saturated.

As we look into His precious face we see evidence of pain and torture. But we can hardly recognize the Victim because of the blood from the deeply imbedded crown of thorns. The Master has now been suspended on the cross for over an hour.

His one dying request, after having asked God to forgive His murderers, was for just a few drops of cool water to cool His throat and tongue. But the hard-hearted, contemptible cowards turn a deaf ear to His plea. Instead, they pass Him a sponge dipped in bitter gall and vinegar.

The human mind will never be able to conceive a more dastardly show of human torture than that displayed by Annas, Caiaphas, Pilate, and the rest of the gang assembled at the foot of that cross, awaiting the temporary death of the Son of God.

Despite all this, the Son of God asked the Father to forgive them because they knew not what they were doing.

What a loving request to make under such circumstances, and it served to magnify the true spirit of eternal forgiveness and unfailing compassion of the Saviour, Jesus Christ.

There in those final moments of transition from life to temporary death, His noble and sweet character had not changed one iota. Though they had broken His heart, there still remained ample room in that heart for a continuance of typical compassion and sympathy as He fervently and reverently prayed for full pardon.

Was He not in a forgiving spirit to the very end? What about the dying thief on the cross who, unlike his companion, asked the Master to remember him when He was in His Paradise? You know the answer —he was saved at that very moment. Even then, the Master could save others from the tormenting and eternal fires of an awful hell.

All is quiet once more. Then Jesus sees His broken-hearted mother standing with John, who is still comforting her in those final moments of distress. Christ said to her, *"Woman, behold thy son!"* Then He turned towards John and said, *"Behold thy mother!"*[181]

Was not that a heart-rending scene? Jesus, in His dying moments, realized that after the resurrection on Sunday morning, there would no longer be the sweet pleasure of companionship with His precious mother. So as His last will and testament, while dying upon the cross, He willed the tender care and affection of His mother into the keeping of the disciple whom He loved.

---

181) John 19:26-27.

This is just another illustration of how perfectly Jesus obeyed every command and wish of God. He well remembered the commandment, *"Honor thy father and thy mother."* As the tinge of death began to supplant the fire of life, He never failed to keep uppermost in His heart and mind the duties and responsibilities of the true Son of God.

Some may wonder why none of the half-brothers of Jesus were present, consoling their own mother in her time of travail. The reason is that none of them believed Jesus to be Divine. It was after the resurrection that His half-brother, James, became a convert. Like so many others, including Thomas, one of the supposedly loyal disciples, they had to see His nail-scarred hands before they would believe.

Turning momentarily back to the cross:

About noontime giant clouds covered the sunshine and created complete darkness, akin to night. Then a curtain seemed to cover over and surround the tragedy of the cross, as if God did not want those cruel men to longer gaze upon the agonizing and dying Son. Then, just as the dark clouds seemed to be breaking, He sensed a feeling of being abandoned by all —and He cried out in a loud voice, *My God, my God, why hast thou forsaken me?*[182]

His exclamation carried a tone of indescribable suffering, as though conscious of desolation. As we think on this sad and lonely part of the fiendish crucifixion, we must keep in mind that Christ, though Divine, was in human form, with a heart and mind of humankind.

---

182) Matthew 27:46 & Mark 15:34. See also Psalm 22:1.

To be sure, it was not a shaking of faith in His Father above, but more of a human expression of desolation as the sweet fellowship with God Almighty was about to be temporarily suspended, until the hour of His miraculous resurrection on Sunday morn.

Then those at the foot of the cross, without faith, and with misunderstanding, said:

> …let us see whether Elias (Elijah) will come
> to take him down. [183]

Jesus was not appealing for Elijah or His Heavenly Father to come *"take Him down"* from that cross. He knew He would see it through. Yet, surely He had every reason to be possessed with a broken heart as He was stretched out on that lonely and rugged cross, dying for the sins of a lost and indifferent world.

Now this inquiry: Have you not been deeply moved by this picture of His human suffering and His Divine Personality—and by the countless cruelties wrongfully inflicted upon Him by those who knew He was guiltless?

This book will be concluded by returning, quietly and reverently, to the foot of that rugged cross to witness the last act of that tragic drama involving the Son of God.

As we approach, the atmosphere had become tense. No longer does anyone speak in cheap derision of the Master, for by now the final insults have been hurled, and the last acts of violence committed. Those who hate Him, still poisoned by their prejudiced hearts, await the moment of His

---

183) Mark 15:36.

expiration, which will be the culmination of their sordid conspiracies and base treachery.

Still not a word of complaint falls from Christ's parched lips. Then He moves His head, slightly, as it is raised Heavenward, and He declares:

> It is finished: [184] Father, into thy hands I commend my spirit: [185]

What a beautiful climax! What a majestic way to terminate world relationships—by commending His Spirit into the hands of God. Oh, what an expression of faith.

Maybe—only conjecture of course—when the earthquake came, and the lightning crashed, and the rocks split in two, and the dead came forth from their graves, it was God's way of showing His displeasure over the cruelties inflicted upon His only begotten Son.

They did not have to be as cruel as they were, even though they were determined to kill Him by crucifixion. There was no need to beat Him, spit in His face, force a crown of thorns upon His brow, and pierce His side. Only corrupt and heartless men would do such a thing.

Let us, in these closing moments, note the significance of those last words of Jesus, *"Father, into thy hands I commend my spirit,"* He proved that He sincerely believed that which He so courageously taught others. This was His reaffirmation of man's only hope for peace unto the soul and the joy of eternal life in the Kingdom of God.

---

184) John 19:30.
185) Luke 23:46.

Now let us consider His statement, *"It is finished."* What, one might rightfully inquire, was "finished?" Those who mistreated and crucified Christ were forever finished:

1. Annas, the conspiring political boss of Judea, whose scheming to destroy Christ failed because of the Lord's glorious resurrection on the third day, just as He had said. Annas lies somewhere in an unmarked grave. The memory of his name is but an abomination.

2. Caiaphas, the discredited and despised high priest, who forever disgraced the office he was wholly unfit to hold, went to his grave with the stain of Christ's blood on his putrid hands, the arch murderer of the Son of God.

3. Judas Iscariot, the traitor who hanged himself on the highway. The worms took care of him. When he took his own life, he could hear the echo of the Master's voice, *"Good were it for that man if he had never been born."*[186]

THE MURDERERS OF THE SON OF GOD

JUDAS   ANNAS   CAIAPHAS   PILATE

HE SANHEDRIN   ROMAN SOLDIERS   THE CRUEL MOB

---

186) Mark 14:21.

4. Pontius Pilate, the moral coward whose conduct toward Jesus was so repulsive that the Emperor, after learning of the crucifixion of Jesus, had him condemned him to die with the stain of guilt upon his depraved heart.

5. Herod Antipas, the king, who, like his father before him, completely discredited the kingship of his domain; and who made sport of humiliating Christ. He lived long enough to talk with the men and women who were eyewitnesses of Jesus being lifted up through the clouds and into Heaven. He lived to regret his conduct in relation to Christ.

6. The Sanhedrin—supposedly the great Supreme Court of the Jews— was abandoned in utter disgrace a short while after the crucifixion of their Holy Victim. Today, after almost two thousand years, the Jews are ashamed of its black record of treachery and infamy.

7. The Pharisees and Sadducees and the group of Roman soldiers who played their vicious parts in the awful drama of the "trials" and crucifixion of Jesus. They faded into the catacombs of forgotten dreams. But the record of their deeds stands indelibly imprinted in the inspired Word of God for all to read.

8. There is now forever finished, and ensconced within the archives of Biblical history, the black record of the unfair, illegal "trials" of the Master, which paint a picture of disgrace and villainy for all to see. For His so-called "trials" were no more than a farce—judicial murder.

In respect to the Son of God, what was *finished?* His final words on Calvary's cross were the solemn pronouncement of His ultimate victory—eternal victory not only over death, but the forces which produce death. Moreover, it was the stamp of finality upon His ministry on this earth as He taught a sin-filled world the way of life eternal.

By His death on the cross, He magnificently finished His noble part in God's plan of Salvation—and He finished it in loyal obedience, meekness, submission and courage; ready and willing to carry out the will of His Father.

His unchanging attitude, His fidelity of purpose, from the childish utterances at the Temple, when only twelve, to the final statement on the crest of Calvary, was summed up in this, *"Not my will, but thine, be done."*[187]

When His part was "finished," there was immediately created eternal hope for man's salvation—the only hope—for life everlasting and peace to the soul.

---

187) See Luke 22:42.

WHAT YOU DON'T KNOW ABOUT CHRIST'S CRUCIFIXION

Christ's illegal trial was quickly followed by His death… but it wasn't any ordinary death. He died by one of the most painful methods known to man.

Back then, people understood the excruciating pain crucifixion caused, but today most people have no idea.

In this 32 page full-color comic, a doctor explains what happens to a body as it is crucified. You will, for the first time, understand the torture Christ suffered, and gain a whole new appreciation for the price He paid for your sins.